RUSSIAN
phrasebook

James Jenkin

Russian Phrasebook
   1st edition

Published by
   Lonely Planet Publications Pty Ltd (A.C.N. 005 607 983)
   PO Box 617, Hawthorn, Victoria, 3122, Australia
   Lonely Planet Publications, Inc
   PO Box 2001A, Berkeley, CA 94702, USA

Printed by
   Singapore National Printers Ltd, Singapore

Published
   December 1991

About this Book
This book was produced from an original manuscript by James Jenkin, with assistance from Kesha Gelbak and Grant Taylor. Sally Steward edited the book and Ann Jeffree was responsible for design and front cover illustration.

National Library of Australia Cataloguing in Publication Data

Jenkin, James
   Russian phrasebook

   ISBN 0 86442 118 4

   1. Russian language – Conversation and phrasebooks – English. I. Title.

   491.783421

© Lonely Planet Publications Pty Ltd, 1991

Contents

Introduction

Russian is the official language of the USSR, and is the first language of the 150 million Russians who live there. It is also spoken to some extent by the remaining 130 million people in the Soviet Union. Russian is, in fact, amongst the four most widely spoken languages in the world, together with Chinese, English and Spanish. Despite demographic variations in the language, the standard Moscow variety is understood by virtually all Russian speakers.

Although its alphabet may look unusual, Russian is, in fact, related to English. Both belong to the Indo-European family of languages. Russian, along with Polish, Czech, and others, belongs to the Slavonic branch, one of the three largest subgroups of Indo-European, the other two being Romance (which includes Italian and French) and Germanic (which includes English).

The fact that Russian and English are distant relations means that you will often find similarities between basic words in the two languages, such as 'three', *tri*, три; 'daughter', *doch'*, дочь, and 'brother', *brat*, брат. Sometimes the relationship is more subtle as in 'house, apartment block', *dom*, дом, which is related to the English word 'domestic', and the '*-grad*' in 'Leningrad' which is actually related to the English 'garden'.

The Russian alphabet was devised quite late, probably around the 9th century, and many letters were taken from Greek. Legend has it that the alphabet was invented by a missionary St Cyril – thus it is named Cyrillic. The alphabet might seem intimidating, but actually a number of letters look and sound similar to letters in English (А, Б (b), Д (d), Е, К, М, О, Т). What is most tricky is not to mispronounce the few that look like English but sound totally different; for example, В is pronounced like a 'v'! Happily, most letters have only one or two possible pronunciations, and this is almost always predictable from the context. It is quite easy to acquire a rough working knowledge of the alphabet, which is handy for reading maps and street signs, and may make you feel a bit more at home. Nevertheless, all Russian words in this book are given with a transliterated equivalent, using a system designed to be accurate, yet easy and quick to read.

Russians do not have a tradition of superficial warmth in public. You may be surprised by offhandedness, or even rudeness, in shops and offices. However, if you are able to break the ice, Russians can change dramatically, showing immense warmth, generosity and openness about personal matters. It is not generally rude to ask how someone's relationship is getting along, or what they think of a political issue, or how their finances are! Since there has not been much contact between Russia and the West, people can be surprised and pleased if you make an effort to speak their language.

This book is about the Russian language and therefore concentrates on the way Russians tend to do things. Nearly half the population of the USSR is not Russian, and in some republics Russian and Russians are not particularly popular. However, this just requires your sensitivity – as far as communication goes, many Soviet citizens have some knowledge of another European language, and you could try getting a phrasebook of the local language.

Don't be shy and you will soon be communicating in Russian! *Fsyevo kharosheva!*

Pronunciation

The Alphabet

Below is the Russian alphabet, followed by the phonetic symbols which this book uses to transliterate Russian letters, along with examples of English words containing similar sounds.

А а	'a' as in father
Б б	'b' as in but
В в	'v' as in van
Г г	'g' as in god
Д д	'd' as in dog
Е е	'ye' as in yet
Ё ё	'yo' as in yonder
Ж ж	'zh' as the 's' in measure
З з	'z' as in zoo
И и	as the English 'i' but stretch your lips, a bit like the 'ee' in see
Й й	'y' as in boy
К к	'k' as in kind
Л л	'l' as in lamp
М м	'm' as in mad
Н н	'n' as in not
О о	'o' as in more (when stressed)
	'a' as in about (when unstressed)
П п	'p' as in pig

Р р	'r' as in rub (but rolled if you can!)
С с	's' as in sing
Т т	't' as in ten
У у	'u' as in pull (**not** as in 'but'!)
Ф ф	'f' as in fan
Х х	'kh' as the 'ch' in Bach
Ц ц	'ts' as in bits
Ч ч	'c' as in chin
Ш ш	'sh' as in shop
Щ щ	'sh' as in sheet
Ъ	a 'hard sign' – means a slight gap between letters (very rare)
Ы	'i' as in 'ill'
Ь	' – a 'soft sign' – means the consonant before it is 'softened' ie pronounced as if there is a very short 'y' sound after it.
Э э	'e' as in end
Ю ю	'yu' as in useful
Я я	'ya' as in yard

Stress

Russian words are strongly stressed on one syllable. Unfortunately, you can't predict which one! So throughout this book stressed syllables are printed in bold. Note that some Russian words sound similar to English words except for the stress. For example, 'taxi' in Russian is pronounced *taksi*, 'tourist' is *turist*.

Intonation

To turn a statement into a question in Russian, you don't have to change the word order at all, but simply change the intonation – how your voice goes up and down when you say the sentence. As a rule, in a statement, your voice stays quite level and then falls on the stressed syllable of the last word (and stays as low). In a question, your voice also stays quite level and then rises very sharply on the stressed syllable of the last word (and then comes back down a bit):

They sell beer. (statement)

Pradayut piva.   Продают пиво.
Do they sell beer? (question)

Pradayut piva?   Продают пиво?

A Note for Users of the *USSR – a travel survival kit*

This phrasebook and Lonely Planet's *USSR – a travel survival kit* use the same transcription system except for some specific differences. The travel survival kit is designed to correspond closely to official Soviet transcriptions (such as place names), while this book concentrates on accuracy of pronunciation. For example, the city Новосибирск is written 'Novosibirsk' in the travel survival kit, which is how it will be written on maps. This book would transliterate it as 'navasibirsk' which is based on how it is pronounced.

The specific differences are:

Russian letter	tsk	phrasebook
е	e	ye
О (unstressed)	o	a
Щ	shch	sh
Ы	y	i
Ь	not written	'
-ие	ie	iye
-ий, -ый	y	iy

In addition, the phrasebook shows changes created by certain combinations of sounds (eg в is normally pronounced 'v' but before a к it sounds like 'f': therefore в Киеве, 'in Kiev', is written *f Kiyevye*).

Grammar

Word Order

Normally you can use English word order in Russian and you will be understood. However, you may notice that Russians will sometimes put the most important or interesting information last in a sentence, as if they were building up to a punch line:

There's milk for sale in the food shop!

v gastranomye pradayotsa malako!

Б гастрономе продаётця молоко!
(lit: In the food shop is for sale milk!)

Verbs

Most simply, verbs can be described as 'doing words' – such as 'We work in a shop', 'She loves vodka'. In English and Russian, you can put endings on a verb to show when this action takes place: present, past or future, eg 'I worked in a shop' is called the 'past tense'.

Present

Russian verbs in the present tense add endings depending on whether I, you, a third person, we, or they are doing whatever it is.

to work   *rabotat'*   работать

This is called the 'dictionary form' – if you look up a verb in the dictionary, like 'work', this is the form you'll find. However, it is also generally a useless form – to use it, you have to drop the ending -ТЬ *(-t')* and put endings on as we discussed earlier.

I work	*ya rabotayu*	я работаю
you work	*vi rabotayetye*	вы работаете
she/he works	*ana/on rabotayet*	ана/он работает
we work	*mi rabotayem*	мы работаем
they work	*ani rabotayut*	они работают

to speak   *gavarit'*   говорить

When you find a dictionary form ending in -ИТЬ *(-it')*, drop the -И *(-i)*, as well as the -ТЬ *(-t')*, and add the endings -Ю *(-yu)*, -ИТЕ *(-itye)*, -ИТ *(-it)*, -ИМ *(-im)* and -ЯТ *(-yat)*.

I speak	*ya gavaryu*	я говорю
you speak	*vi gavaritye*	вы говорите
she/he speaks	*ana/on gavarit*	она/он говорит
we speak	*mi gavarim*	мы говорим
they speak	*ani gavaryat*	они говорят

Some verbs do not follow these patterns exactly but if you use these endings you will be understood.

There is an alternative word for 'you'; TЫ *(ti)*, with its own verb ending -ешь *(-yesh')*; or for the second pattern -ишь *(-ish')*. This is informal and generally only used between good friends or with children and family – therefore all the phrases in this book use the formal *vi*. However, young adults sometimes use *ti* amongst themselves, even with strangers, but it requires some feel before you know whether *ti* will be appropriate. Therefore it is advisable to use the formal *vi* until you are invited to use *ti*. Even Russians sometimes worry about which 'you' to use!

Note that Russian leaves out the verb 'to be' in the present tense ('am', 'is', 'are'). Whereas we would say in English 'That is our bus', Russians just say 'That our bus', *eta nash aftobus*, Это наш автобус.

Past
English can put '-ed' on the end of a verb to show something happened in the past. Russian has an equivalent: -ла *(-la)*. Just drop the ending -ть *(-t')* from the dictionary form first.

to see
    vidyet'   видеть
I saw Leningrad.
    ya vidyela   Я видела
    lyeningrat   Ленинград.

to ask
    sprasit'   спросить
Natasha asked where
the museum is.
    natasha sprasila,   Наташа спросила,
    gdye muzyey   где музей.

The past tense doesn't have a set of endings like the present tense, but you have to drop the -a *(-a)* from the -ла *(-la)* if you are a male.

I (m) saw Leningrad.
    ya vidyel   Я видел
    lyeningrat   Ленинград.
Boris asked where the museum
is.
    baris sprasil, gdye   Борис спросил,
    muzyey   где музей.

After 'we', any other plural, and the formal 'you', вы *(vi)*, you have to change -ла *(-la)*, to -ли *(-li)*.

We saw Leningrad.
    mi vidyeli   Мы видели
    lyeningrat   Ленинград.

The tourists asked where the museum is.

turisti sprasili, gdye muzyey

Туристы спросили, где музей.

To Be

Remember that although Russian doesn't use 'to be' in the present tense, it has a regular past tense – but note the -ла *(-la)* is stressed, but the plural -ли *(-li)* is not.

to be

bit'

быть

Natasha was there. Natasha has been there.

natasha bila tam

Наташа была там.

We were there. We have been there.

mi bili tam

Мы были там.

To Have

Russian doesn't usually use a verb meaning 'to have' – you have to learn the following expressions, which roughly mean 'With me exists ...'

I have ...

u myenya yest' ...

У меня есть ...

Do you have ...?

u vas yest' ...?

У вас есть ...?

We have ...

u nas yest' ...

У нас есть ...

If you don't have something, the following expression is very useful:

I don't have one/We don't have
any/There aren't any/ etc.
   nyetu   Нету.

Future
English sometimes uses the future tense, 'will' + verb, but almost always uses the present tense to refer to what you intend to do, eg 'I'm working tomorrow'. The future is obvious from the context, especially the word 'tomorrow'. Russian is similar: it often uses the present tense to refer to the future:

I'm working tomorrow.
   ya rabotayu zaftra   Я работаю завтра.

Modals
This is a term for when you want to modify a verb by saying, for instance, you can, or want to, or should do something, eg 'I want to buy badges'.

In Russian, the verb following a modal is always just in the dictionary form:

buy (dictionary form)
   pakupat'   покупать
I buy
   ya pakupayu   я покупаю

But:

I want to buy
   ya khachu pakupat'
   (**not** *pakupayu*)   Я хочу покупать

Can

In English, 'can' usually expresses ability.

I can ...
   ya magu ...   Я могу ...
I can't ...
   ya nye magu ...   Я не могу ...
Can you ...?
   vi mozhetye ...?   Вы можете ...?

In colloquial English, 'can' sometimes replaces 'may' to express being allowed to do something.

Can I (take photos?)
   mozhna mnye   Можно мне (фото
   (fatagrafiravat')?   графировать)?
You're not allowed to ...
   vam nyel'zya ...   Вам нельзя ...

These two words *mozhna*, можно, and *nyel'zya*, нельзя, can be used on their own, as in the following typical Soviet conversation:

May I?
   mozhna?   Можно?
No you may not.
   nyel'zya   Нельзя.

Want

I want to (know)
  ya khachu (znat')
                 Я хочу (знать)

I would like to ... (more polite)
  ya khatyela bi ...(f)/
  ya khatyel bi ...(m)
                 Я хотела бы ...(f)/
                 Я хотел бы...(m)

Would you like to ...
  vi khatyeli bi ...?
                 Вы хотели бы ...?

I don't want to ...
  ya nye khachu ...
                 Я не хочу ...

Must, Have To

I have to (go)
  mnye nuzhna (itti)
                 Мне нужно (идти)

Do you have to ...?
  vam nuzhna ...?
                 Вам нужно ...?

Negatives

To say you are not doing something, Russian simply puts не *(nye)* before the verb. This is simpler than English, which sometimes has to put in other words as well (like 'do'), as you can see in the following examples.

She works here.
  ana rabotayet zdyes'
                 Она работает здесь.

She doesn't work here.
  ana nye rabotayet zdyes'
                 Она не работает здесь.

I like wine.
ya lyublyu vino   Я люблю вино.
I don't like wine.
ya nye lyublyu vino   Я не люблю вино.

Articles

Russian does not have articles ('the' and 'a'). Remembering that Russian does not use the verb 'to be' in the present tense either, the English sentence 'I am a tourist' will simply become 'I tourist' *ya turist*, Я турист.

Nouns
Plurals

The most common plural ending is -ы *(-i)*, and will always be understood. Note that nouns ending in -a *(-a)* replace the -a *(-a)* with the -ы *(-i)*.

That is a shop.
eta magazin   Это магазин.
Those are shops.
eta magazini   Это магазины.

But:

That is a flat.
eta kvartira   Это квартира.
Those are flats.
eta kvartiri   Это квартиры.

Note that the word Это... *(eta ...)*, stays the same whether you are pointing out one thing or several things; it can mean 'This is ...', 'That is ...', 'These are ...' or 'Those are ...'

Location
Note that after 'in/at', в *(v)*, and 'on/by (train etc)', на *(na)*, you have to put -е *(-ye)* ,on the end of the word afterwards (or if there is already a vowel on the end you have to replace it):

restaurant
ryestaran   ресторан
I was at the restaurant.
ya bila v ryestaranye Я была в ресторане.

But:

car
mashina   машина
She is in the car.
ana v mashinye   Она в машине.

Accusative Case
Many verbs involve doing something to something. 'I am painting my house' means the house is having something done to it – it is being painted. 'My sister bought a record' means the record had something done to it – it got bought. A noun having something done to it is said to be in the 'accusative case'. In Russian, if a noun ends in -а *(-a)*, in the accusative case you have to change this to -у *(-u)*.

newspaper
gazeta газета

I bought a newspaper.
ya kupila gazyetu Я купила газету.

Moscow
maskva Москва

We saw Moscow.
mi vidyeli maskvu Мы видели Москву.

This rule does *not* apply after the 'have' expressions described earlier:

car
mashina машина

I have a car.
u myenya yest' mashina У меня есть машина.
(not *mashinu* машину)

Adjectives & Adverbs
Adjectives

When you look up an adjective (a word which describes a noun, like 'wonderful', 'expensive', 'interesting') in the dictionary, it will usually end in -ый *(-iy)*, or occasionally in -ий *(-iy)*, or -ой *(-oy)*. Just remember that when it describes a noun ending in -a *(-a)*, you must change the adjective ending to -ая *(-aya)*.

That is a wonderful view.
eta pryekrasniy vit
Это прекрасный вид.

The room is expensive.
nomyer daragoy
Номер дорогой.

He is interesting.
on intyeryesniy
Он интересный.

But:

That is a wonderful street.
*eta pryekrasnaya
ulitsa*
Это прекрасная
улица.

The book is expensive.
kniga daragaya
Книга дорогая.

She is interesting.
ana intyeryesnaya
Она интересная.

Possessive Adjectives

Words like 'my', 'your' etc, sometimes also have an alternative
form if they go with a word ending in -a *(-a)*:

my	*moy/maya*	мой/моя
your	*vash/vasha*	ваш/ваша
your (informal)	*tvoy/tvaya*	твой/твоя
her	*yeyo*	её
his	*yevo*	его
our	*nash/nasha*	наш/наша
their	*ikh*	их

Adverbs

Something Russians use often on adjectives is the simple ending

-o (pronounced -*a* when unstressed, which is in most cases). This is the adverb ending, like English '-ly'. An adverb doesn't describe a person or thing, but describes how someone does something. Note the adverb usually comes second in Russian.

He is a wonderful guide.
(adjective – describes the guide)
  on pryekrasniy gid   Он прекрасный гид.
He speaks English wonderfully.
(adverb – describes how he
speaks)
  on pryekrasna gavarit   Он прекрасно говорит
  pa angliyski   по-английски.

The ending -o has further uses – you can use it just to refer to a state of affairs without having to name any particular object:

Wonderful! That's wonderful!
  pryekrasna!   Прекрасно!
How expensive!
  doraga!   Дорого!
This is really interesting!
  intyeryesna!   Интересно!
It's cold.
  kholadna   Холодно.
Good.
  kharasho   Хорошо.

These one-word sentences are perfectly acceptable and very common in Russian.

Questions

Like English, Russian has a number of small question words with which you can start a sentence.

what	*shto*	что
who	*kto*	кто
why	*pachyemu*	почему
when	*kagda*	когда
where	*gdye*	где
where (to)	*kuda*	куда

Use this last one when you're talking about going somewhere:

Where are you going?
   kuda vi idyotye?   Куда вы идёте?

Note that after question words you don't change the sentence around (as you do in English), you just leave it as it was.

You are working.
   vi rabotayetye.   Вы работаете.
Where are you working?
   gdye vi rabotayetye?   Где вы работаете?

In addition, as we read in the section on 'Intonation' in the Pronunciation chapter, Russian does not change the word order for a question without a question word either, but has a sharp rise on the last word.

   If you don't feel confident about using intonation, you can put да? *(da?)*, (literally 'yes?') on the end of a statement, equivalent to English expressions such as 'aren't you?', 'isn't it?' etc:

That's the Kremlin, isn't it?
 eta kryeml', da?   Это Кремль, да?

Some Useful Words

and	*i*	и
at	*v*	в
because	*patamu shto*	потому что
because of	*iz za*	из-за
but	*no*	но
by (train etc)	*na*	на
for	*dlya*	для
here	*zdyes'*	здесь
in	*v*	в
on	*na*	на
near	*okala*	около
there	*tam*	там

Greetings & Civilities

Greetings

Russian has an all-purpose greeting like English 'hello' –
zdrazdvitye!, Здравствуйте! It can be used at any time of
day, and both between friends and when being formally introduced. Russians tend to shake hands when they greet each other.
Other more specific (and less common) greetings include:

Good morning.
   dobraye utra   Доброе утро.
Good afternoon.
   dobriy dyen'   Добрый день.
Good evening.
   dobriy vyechyer   Добрый вечер.

Asking 'How are you?' sounds a bit un-Russian – as a rule,
zdrazdvitye, Здравствуйте, covers 'Hello/How are you?/
How do you do?' However, if you are on friendly terms with
someone, you can get them to talk about what's been happening
with something like:

How are things?
   kag dyela?   Как дела?
How's life?
   kag zhizn'?   Как жизнь?
What's new?
   shto novava?   Что нового?

Possible answers include:

Fine, thank you.
  spasiba, kharasho   Спасибо, хорошо.
Not bad.
  nichyevo   Ничего.
There's nothing new.
  nichyevo novava nyet   Ничего нового нет.
And with you?
  a u vas?   А у вас?

Attracting Someone's Attention

The Russian equivalent of 'Excuse me, please' is *izvinitye, pazhalsta*, Извините, пожалуйста. However, if you are attracting someone's attention in order to ask a question, the usual expression is 'Tell me, please ...', *skazhitye, pazhalsta*, Скажите, пожалуйста.

To enter somewhere like an office it is polite to ask 'May I?', *mozhna?*, Можно?, or 'I'm not disturbing you?', *ya vam nye myeshayu?*, Я вам не мешаю?.

Goodbyes

Goodbye.
  dasvidanya   До свидания.
  shasliva (more informal   Счастливо.
  but common)
See you tomorrow.
  dazaftra   До завтра.

It was very nice (to meet you).

bila ochyen' priyatna (paznakomit'sa s vami)

Было очень приятно (познакомиться с вами).

I hope we see each other soon.

nadyeyus', shta skora uvidimsa

Надеюсь, что скоро увидимся.

Sorry, but I have to get going.

izvinitye, pazhalsta, mnye para iti

Извините, пожалуйста, мне пора идти.

Say hello to your husband/ your wife.

pyeryedaytye privyet vashemu muzhu/ vashey zhenye

Передайте привет вашему мужу / вашей жене.

Good night.

spakoynay nochi!

Спокойной ночи!

Civilities

Please.
pazhalsta — Пожалуйста.

Thank you (very much).
spasiba (bal'shoye) — Спасибо (большое).

Thank you very much for all
your trouble.
spasiba za fsye — Спасибо за все
vashi khlopati — ваши хлопоты.

If someone thanks you, you should say *pazhalsta*, пожалуйста,
in return. We saw above that this means 'please', but – very
importantly – it's also used for 'Don't mention it/That's all right'.
Russians also use *pazhalsta*, пожалуйста, when they hand
you something. In this context you might also hear (literally) 'to
your health', *na zdarovye*, на здоровье.

Apologies

Sorry.
prastitye, pazhalsta — Простите, пожалуйста.

Sorry? (What did you say?)
prastitye? — Простите?
(shto vi skazali?) — (Что вы сказали?)

Excuse me.
izvinitye, pazhalsta — Извините, пожалуйста.

Excuse me. (When trying to
get past)
prapustitye, pazhalsta — Пропустите,
пожалуйста.

I didn't mean to.
ya eta sluchayna

Я это случайно.

That's all right/It doesn't matter.
nichyevo

Ничего!

Don't worry.
nye byespakoytyes'!

Не беспокойтесь!

Small Talk

Help!
Language Difficulties

An expression well worth memorising:

Could you please write that
down?
    zapishitye eta,
    pazhalsta!   Запишите это,
                      пожалуйста!

You may find this useful whenever you need to know any little bit
of precise information – like a price, a time or an address. Other
expressions that may help you if you don't understand are:

What does that mean?
    shto eta znachit?   Что это значит?
Sorry, what did you say?
    prastitye, shto vi
    skazali?   Простите, что вы
                      сказали?
Could you please speak more
slowly?
    gavaritye pamyedlyenyeye, Говорите помедленее,
    pazhalsta   пожалуйста.
Just a minute!
(eg while you look something
up)
    minutachku!   Минуточку!

I understand.
  ya panimayu   Я понимаю.
I see.
  panyatna   Понятно.
I don't understand.
  ya nye panimayu   Я не понимаю.
Can you show me?
  pakazhitye,   Покажите,
  pazhalsta   пожалуйста.
I'll show you.
  ya vam pakazhu   Я вам покажу.

If you are having real problems (it may be because many people in the USSR only speak Russian as a second language) you can always try:

Do you speak ...?
  vi gavarltye ...?   Вы говорите ...?
Does anyone speak ...?
  kto nibud' gavarit ...?   Кто-нибудь говорит ...?
    English
      pa angliyski   по-английски
    French
      pa frantsuski   по-французски
    German
      pa nyemyetski   по-немецки
    Japanese
      pa yaponski   по-японски
    Spanish
      pa ispanski   по-испански

Top 13 Useful Phrases

The following are all-purpose expressions that you might need on the spur of the moment.

May I?/Do you mind?/Is it all right?
    mozhna?   Можно?

Yes.
    da   Да.

No.
    nyet   Нет.

Hello!/How do you do?
    zdrastvitye!   Здравствуйте!

Good bye!
    dasvidanya!   До свидания!

Thank you.
    spasiba   Спасибо.

Please/Don't mention it.
(after 'Thank you')
    pazhalsta   Пожалуйста.

Excuse me/Sorry!	
prastitye, pazhalsta!	Простите, пожалуйста!
It doesn't matter/That's all right.	
nichyevo!	Ничего!
I am (a tourist/Susan).	
ya (turist/Suzan)	Я (турист/Сузан)
What's that?	
shto eta?	Что это?
Where is (the toilet)?	
gdye (tualyet)?	Где (туалет)?
How much?	
skol'ka?	Сколько?

Don't be shy about talking to people in the USSR! Russians will be very open concerning anything from politics to how much they earn.

Meeting People

What is your name?	
kak vas zavut?	Как вас зовут?
My name is ...	
myenya zavut	Меня зовут...
I am ...	
ya ...	Я ...

To be very friendly and informal, you can use your first name, as in English.

My name is Anna.	
myenya zavut ana	Меня зовут Анна.

Or to be more formal you can use the Russian word for Mrs/Ms/Miss, *gaspazha*, госпожа, or Mr, *gaspadin*, господин, with your surname to refer to yourself and other non-Russians.

I am Mrs Clarke.
   ya gaspazha klark   Я госпожа Кларк.

However, Russians do not use these words for themselves. Instead they use their first name with their patronymic, a second name taken from their father's first name (so try to remember both names when you are introduced!).

My name is Irina Pavlovna.
(Irina, daughter of Pavel)
   myenya zavut irina   Меня зовут Ирина
   pavlavna   Павловна.

Hello, Boris Ivanich. (Boris, son of Ivan)
   zdrazdviytye,   Здравствуйте,
   baris ivanich   Борис Иванович!

If you're not sure what to call someone, you can always ask: 'What should I call you?' *kak mnye vas nazvat'?* Как мне вас назвать?

This is ...
  eta ...   Это ...
    my colleague
      maya kalyega (f)   моя коллега (f)
      moy kalyega (m)   мой коллега (m)
    my (female, girl-) friend
      maya padruga   моя подруга
    my (male, boy-) friend
      moy druk   мой друг
    my husband
      moy mush   мой муж
    my wife
      maya zhena   моя жена

If you have been introduced, shake hands and say 'It's very nice.' – it's understood you mean 'to meet you' – *ochyen' priyatna*, очень приятно. Russians of both sexes shake hands a lot – if you see someone again, it's polite to shake their hand again.

Nationalities

Where are you from?
atkuda vi?   Откуда вы?

I'm from ...
ya iz ...   Я из ...

    Africa
      afriki   Африки

    Australia
      afstralii   Австралии

    Asia
      azii   Азии

    Canada
      kanadi   Канады

    China
      kitaya   Китая

    Denmark
      dani   Дании

    England
      anglii   Англии

    Europe
      yevropi   Европы

    Finland
      finlandii   Финляндии

    France
      frantsii   Франции

    Germany
      gyermanii   Германии

    Holland
      golandii   Голландии

Hong Kong		
gonkonga		Гонконга
India		
indii		Индии
Ireland		
irlandii		Ирландии
Israel		
izrailya		Израил
Italy		
italii		Италии
Japan		
yaponii		Японии
Middle East		
sryednyeva vastoka		Среднего востока
New Zealand		
novay zyelandii		Новой Зеландии
Norway		
narvyegii		Норвегии
Scotland		
shatlandii		Шотландии
Singapore		
singapura		Сингапура
South America		
yuzhnay amyeriki		Южной Америки
Spain		
ispanii		Испании
Sweden		
shvyetsii		Швеции
Switzerland		
shvyetsarii		Швецарии
USA		
amyeriki		Америки

There are over 100 nationalities in the Soviet Union, many of which are not Slavic at all. Russia is only one (albeit the largest) of the republics in the USSR. Therefore you could ask:

What republic are you from?
vi is kakoy ryespubliki?
Вы из какой республики?

What city are you from?
vi is kakova gorada?
Вы из какого города?

Where is that?
gdye eta?
Где это?

Please show me.
pakazhitye, pazhalsta
Покажите, пожалуйста.

Age

How old are you?
skol'ka vam lyet?
Сколько вам лет?

I am ... years old.
mnye ... lyet
Мне ... лет.

    18
      vasyemnatsat'
восемнадцать

    25
      dvatsat' pyat'
двадцать пять

Occupations

What do you work as?
kyem vi rabotayetye?
Кем вы работаете?

I'm a/an ...
  ya ...   Я ...
    artist
      khudozhnitsa (f)   художница (f)
      khudozhnik (m)   художник (m)
    business person
      kamyersant   коммерсант
    doctor
      vrach   врач
    driver (bus, taxi, truck)
      vadityel'   водитель
    engineer (a particularly
    prestigious profession in
    the USSR)
      inzhenyer   инженер
    factory worker, manual
    labourer
      rabochaya (f)   рабоча (f)
      rabochiy (m)   рабочий (m)
    journalist
      zhurnalist   журналист

lawyer
advakat — адвокат

mechanic
myekhanik — механик

musician
muzikant — музыкант

nurse
myetsyestra — медсестра

office worker
sluzhashaya (f) — служащая (f)
sluzhashiy (m) — служащий (m)

scientist
uchyonaya (f) — учёная (f)
uchyoniy (m) — учёный (m)

secretary
syekryetarsha (f) — секретарша (f)
syekryetar' (m) — секретарь (m)

student
studyentka (f) — студентка (f)
studyent (m) — студент (m)

teacher
uchityel'nitsa (f) — учительница (f)
uchityel' (m) — учитель (m)

waiter
afitsiant — официант

waitress
afitsiantka — официантка

writer
pisatyel'nitsa (f) — писательница (f)
pisatyel' (m) — писатель (m)

Where do you work?
gdye vi rabotayetye?   Где вы работаете?

I work ...
ya pabotayu ...   Я работаю
   for the army
      varmii   в армии
   for a bank
      v bankye   в банке
   for a company
      f firmye   в фирме
   in a factory
      na zavodye   на заводе
   for the government
      v gasudarstvyenam   в государственном
      uchryezhdyenii   учреждении
   at home
      doma   дома
   in a hospital
      v bal'nitse   в больнице
   in a library
      v bibliatyekye   в библиотеке
   in a school
      f shkolye   в школе
   in a university
      v univyersityetye   в университете

I've come here ...
ya priyekhala syuda (f)   Я приехала сюда (f)
ya priyekhal syuda (m)   Я приехал сюда (m)
   on business
      padyelam   по делам

on holiday
  votpusk   в отпуск
to learn Russian
  uchit'sa ruskamu   учиться
  yaziku   русскому зыку
to study
  uchit'sa   учиться
to work
  rabotat'   работать

Religion

What is your religion?
  kakaya vasha ryeligiya?   Какая ваша религия?

I am ...
  ya ...   Я ...
  Buddhist
    budistka (f)   будистка (f)
    budist (m)   будист (m)
  Catholic
    katolichka (f)   католичка (f)
    katolik (m)   католик (m)

Christian
khristianka (f)   христианка(f)
khristianin (m)   христианин (m)
Hindu
induska (f)   индуска (f)
indus (m)   индус (m)
Jewish
yevryeyka (f)   еврейка (f)
yevryey (m)   еврей (m)
Muslim
musul'manka (f)   мусульманка (f)
musul'manin (m)   мусульманин(m)
Orthodox
pravaslavnaya (f)   православная (f)
pravaslavniy (m)   православный (m)
not religious
nyevyeruyushaya (f)   неверующая (f)
nyevyeruyushiy (m)   неверующий (m)

Family

Are you married?
  (to a woman) *vi zamuzhem?*   Вы замужем?
  (to a man) *vi zhenat?*   Вы женат?
I am single.
  ya nye zamuzhem (f)   Я не замужем. (f)
  ya nye zhenat (m)   Я не женат. (m)
How many children do you have?
  skol'ka u vas dyetyey?   Сколько у вас детей?

I don't have any children.
dyetyey u myenya nyet

Детей у меня нет.

I have a daughter/son.
*u myenya yest'
doch'/sin*

У меня есть
дочь/сын.

How many brothers/sisters do
you have?
*skol'ka u vas
brat' yef/syestyor?*

Сколько у вас
братьев/сестёр?

Is your husband/wife here?
*vash mush/vasha
zhena zdyes'?*

Ваш муж/ваша
жена здесь?

Do you have a boyfriend/
girlfriend?
*u vas yest' druk/
padruga?*

У вас есть друг/
подруга?

Some Useful Words

aunt
tyotya — тётя

brother
brat — брат

children
dyeti — дети

daughter
doch' — дочь

family
syem'ya — семья

father
papa — папа
atyets (formal) — отец

grandfather
dyedushka — дедушка

grandmother
babushka — бабушка

husband
mush — муж

mother
mama — мама
mat' (formal) — мать

sister
syestra — сестра

son
sin — сын

uncle
dyadya — дядя

wife
zhena — жена

Expressing Feelings

I am ...

angry
    ya syerditaya (f)   Я сердитая. (f)
    ya syerditiy (m)   Я сердитый. (m)

cold
    mnye kholadna   Мне холодно.

grateful
    ya blagadarna (f)   Я благодарна. (f)
    ya blagadaryen (m)   Я благодарен. (m)

happy
    mnye vyesyela   Мне весело.

hot
    mnye zharka   Мне жарко.

hungry
    ya khachu yest'   Я хочу есть.

in a hurry
    ya spyeshu   Я спешу.

right
    ya prava (f)   Я права. (f)
    ya praf (m)   Я прав. (m)

sleepy
    ya khachu spat'   Я хочу спать.

sorry (condolence)	
mnye ochyen' zhal'	Мне очень жаль.
thirsty	
ya khachu pit'	Я хочу пить.
tired	
ya ustala (f)	Я устала. (f)
ya ustal (m)	Я устал. (m)
uncomfortable	
mnye nyeudobna	Мне неудобно.

Opinions

It is a time of big changes in the USSR, and you will have opportunities to argue about everything!

Do you like ...?	
vam nravitsa ...?	Вам нравится ...?
I (really) like ...	
mnye (ochyen')	Мне (очень) нравится ...
nravitsa ...	
I don't (really) like ...	
mnye nye (ochyen')	Мне не (очень)
nravitsa ...	нравится ...
that building	
eta zdaniye	это здание
your city	
vash gorad	ваш город
your country	
vasha rodina	ваша родина
this film	
etat fil'm	этот фильм

Gorbachev	
garbachyof	Горбачёв
her	
ana *	она
him	
on *	он
this music	
eta muzika	эта музыка
the service	
apsluzhivaniye	обслуживание
this / that	
eta *	это

Look up anything in the vocabulary that you like or dislike, and slot it in! Note that the words above with an asterisk should come at the start of the sentence, not the end.

Yes!	
da!	Да!
I agree!	
saglasna! (f)	Согласна! (f)
saglasyen! (m)	Согласен! (m)
No!	
nyet!	Нет!
I'm afraid I don't agree.	
ya bayus', shto	Я боюсь, что я
ya nye saglasna (f)/	не согласна (f)/
saglasyen (m)	согласен (m).
Do you agree?	
vi saglasni?	Вы согласны?

Interests

What do you do in your spare
time?

kak vi pravoditye svayo svabodnaya vryemya?	Как вы проводите своё свободное время?

I like ...
    ya lyublyu ...   Я люблю ...
Do you like ...?
    vi lyubitye ...?   Вы любите ...?

    films
      kino   кино
    football
      futbol   футбол
    music
      muziku   музыку
    reading
      chitat'   читать
    seeing ...
      vidyet' ...   видеть ...
    (going) shopping
      abkhadit' pa magazinam   обходить по магазинам
    travelling
      putyeshestvavat'   путешествовать
    watching TV
      smatryet' tyelyevizar   смотреть теле-визор

I play ...
  ya igrayu ...   Я играю ...
Do you play ...
  vi igrayetye ...?   Вы играете ...?
    cards
      karti   в карты
    chess
      f shakhmati   в шахматы
    football
      f futbol   в футбол
    guitar
      na gitarye   на гитаре
    in an orchestra
      varkyestrye   в оркестре
    piano
      na pianina   на пианино
    in a team
      f kamandye   в команде

Let's go (to a disco)!
  paydyomtye   Пойдёмте
  (v diskatyeku)!   (в дискотеку)!
Let's play (cards)!
  davaytye igrat'   Давайте играть
  (f karti)!   (в карты)!
Let's give it a try!
  paprobuyem!   Попробуем!
Let's!
  davaytye!   Давайте!

Getting Around

Finding Your Way

How do I get to ...?
kak mnye papast' v ...?   Как мне попасть в ...?

Where is ...?
gdye ...?   Где ...?

    the bus station
        aftobusnaya stantsiya   автобусная
        станция

    the train station
        vagzal   вокзал

    the airport
        aeraport   аэропорт

    the subway station
        stantsiya myetro   станция метро

    the ticket office
        kassa   касса

Buying Tickets

As with accommodation, travel arrangements
are normally booked through *Intourist*, the official Soviet tourist agency, but this is changing.
Travel within the USSR can be remarkably
cheap. Note that at metro stations you can buy
a monthly ticket for public transport, *yediniy
bilyet*, единый билет.

52

Ticket Office/Tickets	
kassa/bilyeti	КАССА/БИЛЕТЫ
Information	
spravachnaye	СПРАВОЧНОЕ
byuro/sprafki/	БЮРО/СПРАВКИ/
infarmatsiya	ИНФОРМАЦИЯ

Excuse me, where is the ticket office/information desk?
skazhitye, pazhalsta, Скажите, пожалуйста,
gdye kassa/ где касса/
spravachnaye byuro? справочное бюро?

How much is ...?
skol'ka stoit ...? Сколько стоит ...?

I'd like ...
daytye, pazhalsta   Дайте, пожалуйста, ...

one ticket (to Leningrad)
    adin bilyet   один билет
    v lyeningrat)   (в Ленинград)

two tickets
    dva bilyeta   два билета

a reservation
    platskartu   плацкарту

single (one way)
    vadin kanyets   в один конец

return (round trip)
    tuda i abratna   туда и обратно

economy (aeroplane)
    turistskiy klass   туристский класс

economy (train)
    kupeyniy   купейный

Air

Even to book an internal flight, you will need to have your passport and a visa for the city you are flying to, and you'll have to pay in hard currency at Aeroflot's own exchange rate. However, at the airport, before your flight, just go to the Intourist lounge where they will look after all formalities.

Registration
    ryegistratsiya   РЕГИСТРАЦИЯ

Departures
    atlyot/vilyet   ОТЛЕТ/ВЫЛЕТ

Luggage Pick-up
vidacha bagazha

ВЫДАЧА БАГАЖА

To City
vikhad v gorat

(ВЫХОД) В ГОРОД

Is there a flight to (Omsk)?
yest' li ryeys v (omsk)?

Есть ли рейс в (Омск)?

When is the next flight (to Leningrad)?
kagda slyeduyushiy samalyot (v lyeningrat)?

Когда следующий самолёт (в Ленинград)?

What is the flight number?
kakoy nomyer ryeysa?

Какой номер рейса?

Where do we check in?
gdye ryegistratsiya?

Где регистрация?

When do we have to check in?
kagda nuzhna bit' v erapartu?

Когда нужно быть в аэропорту?

One hour/Two hours before the flight.
za chas/za dva chasa da vilyeta

За час/За два часа до былета.

Where do you check in/pick up luggage?
gdye zdat'/paluchit' bagash?

Где сдать/ получить багаж?

Could I please have (a) ...?
prinyesitye,　　　　　　　　Принесите,
pazhalsta ...?　　　　　　　пожалуйста, ...?
　　cup of coffee
　　　chashku kofi　　　　чашку кофе
　　cup of tea
　　　chashku chayu　　　чашку чаю
　　glass of water
　　　stakan vadi　　　　стакан воды

I feel sick.
　myenya tashnit　　　　　Меня тошнит.

Train

Note that dining cars are rare and it is wise to bring your own food on longer trips. Sharing food can become quite a social event.

Timetable
　raspisaniye　　　　　　　РАСПИСАНИЕ
To Trains
　k payezdam　　　　　　　К ПОЕЗДАМ
To Platforms
　k pyerronam　　　　　　　К ПЕРРОНАМ
Arrivals
　pribitiye　　　　　　　　ПРИБЫТИЕ
Departures
　atpravlyeniye　　　　　ОТПРАВЛЕНИЕ
Platform
　platforma　　　　　　　　ПЛАТФОРМА

Which train goes to
(Leningrad)?
  *kakoy poyezd idyot
  v (lyeningrat)?*

Какой поезд идёт
в (Ленинград)?

Does this train go to (Novosibirsk)?
  *etat poyezd idyot
  v (navasibirsk)?*

Этот поезд идёт
в (Новосибирск)?

Do I need to change?
  *nuzhna dyelat'
  pyeryesatku?*

Нужно делать
пересадку?

When does the train leave?
  *kagda otpravlyayetsa
  poyezd?*

Когда отправляется
поезд?

What is this station called?
  *kak nazivayetsa
  eta stantsiya?*

Как называется
эта станция?

What is the next station?
  *kakaya slyeduyushaya
  stantsiya?*

Какая следующая
станция?

Metro

The older metro stations are amazing and trains run from 6 am until 1 am, at some times of the day every two minutes. To get into the metro you simply put a coin in the turnstile, and you can stay on the system as long as you like.

Change (ie for coins)
   razmyen   РАЗМЕН
This Way To
(Circular Line)
   pyeryekhod na   ПЕРЕХОД НА
   (kol'tsevuyu liniyu)   (КОЛЬЦЕВУЮ ЛИНИЮ)
Way Out
   vikhad v gorad   ВЫХОД В ГОРОД

Which line takes me to ...?
   kakaya liniya idyot v ...?   Какая линия идёт в ...?

Bus, Tram & Trolleybus

You generally have to buy a strip of tickets, and when you enter the vehicle you punch one ticket in a machine on the wall. If it's crowded, you can ask someone else to punch it for you.

Please, punch my ticket!

   kampastiruytye,   Компостируйте,
   pazhalsta!   пожалуйста!

Signs
Bus   А
Trolleybus/Tram   Т/Ш

Which ... goes to
(the Hotel Bukharest)?
  *kakoy ... idyot do
  (gastinitsi bukharyest)?*
    bus
      aftobus
    minibus (usually red)
      marshrutnaye taksi
    tram
      tramvay
    trolleybus
      tralyeybus

Какой ... идёт до
(гостиницы Бухарест)?
автобус
маршрутное такси
трамвай
троллейбус

Please let me know when I
have to get off.
  *pazhalsta,
  pryedupryeditye myenya,
  kagda mnye
  nuzhna vikhadit'.*
What is the next stop?
  *kakaya slyed
  uyushaya astanofka?*

Пожалуйста,
предупредите меня,
когда мне
нужно выходить.

Какая следующая
остановка?

To squeeze past people to get off:

Excuse me while I get past!
  *prapustitye,
  pazhalsta!*
Are you getting off here?
  vi vikhoditye?

Пропустите,
пожалуйста!

Вы выходите?

Taxi

There are state-run and private, cooperative, taxis. Most state-run taxis are yellow with a chequered line along the side. Private taxis will have some sort of sign on them. Non-taxi drivers may stop and offer to drive you as well. For any of these you usually have to negotiate a price at the beginning.

Taxis
  taksi   ТАКСИ
Are you free?
  svabodni?   Свободны?

Could you take me to ...?
  do ... nye davyezyotye?   До ... не довезёте?
    this address
      etava adryesa   этого адреса
    (Sheremetevo) Airport
      eraporta   аэропорта
      sheryemyet'yeva   (Шереметьево)
    central bank
      sentral'nava banka   центрального
                                     банка
    Australian/British/US
    Embassy
      afstraliyskava/   австралийского/
      britanskava/   британского/
      amyerikanskava   американского
      pasol'stva   посольства
    (Rossia) Hotel
      gastinitsi (rassiya)   гостиницы (Россия)

market
  rinka   рынка
post office
  glafpachtamta   главпочтамта
shops
  magazinav   магазинов
(Dinamo) Stadium
  stadiona (dinama)   стадиона (Динамо)
(Park Kultury) Station
  stantsi   станции
  (park kul'turi)   (Парк культуры)
(Pushkin) St
  ulitsi (pushkina)   улицы (Пушкина)

Please slow down.
  zamyedlitye khod,   Замедлите ход,
  pazhalsta!   пожалуйста!
Please stop here.
  astanavityes' zdyes',   Остановитесь здесь,
  pazhalsta   пожалуйста.
Please wait for a minute.
  padazhditye,   Подождите,
  pazhalsta, minutachku   пожалуйста,
                                минуточку.

How much do I owe you?
  skol'ka s myenya?   Сколько с меня?

On Foot

Russian drivers are scary and by law you must cross a major road at a crossing/subway, *pyeryekhod,* ПЕРЕХОД, or a zebra crossing. Note, however, that a zebra crossing just indicates where you are allowed to cross, but you must give way to drivers!

Excuse me, where is ...?
  skazhitye, pazhalsta,   Скажите,
  gdye ...?   пожалуйста, где ...?
    the nearest bank
      blizhayshiy bank   ближайший банк
    a bar
      bar   бар
    a bus stop
      astanofka aftobusa   остановка автобуса

    a church
      tserkav'   церковь
    the nearest department
    store
      blizhayshiy   ближайший
      univyermag   универмаг

the (Ukraina) Hotel	
gastinitsa (ukraina)	гостиница (Украина)
an information booth	
spravachnaye byuro	справочное бюро
a mosque	
myechyet'	мечеть
the main post office	
glafpachtamt	главпочтамт
a restaurant	
ryestaran	ресторан
a snack bar	
zakusachnaya	закусочная
a metro station	
stantsiya myetro	станция метро
a swimming pool	
baseyn	бассейн
a synagogue	
sinagoga	синагога
a taxi rank	
stayanka taksi	стоянка такси

Directions & Instructions

Is it nearby?	
bliska?	Близко?
Is it far?	
dalyeko?	Далеко?
Can I walk there?	
mozhna iti tuda	Можно идти туда
pyeshkom?	пешком?

Can you show me on the map?
pakazhitye mnye na
kartye, pazhalsta
Покажите мне на
карте, пожалуйста.

How many minutes?
skol'ka minut?
Сколько минут?

Go straight ahead.
iditye pryama
Идите прямо.

Turn left ...
pavyernitye nalyeva ...
Поверните налево ...

Turn right ...
pavyernitye naprava ...
Поверните направо ...

    at the corner
      zaugal
      за угол

    at the traffic lights
      u svyetafora
      у светофора

What ... is this?
kak nazivayetsa ...?
Как называется ...?

    street
      eta ulitsa
      эта улица

    suburb
      etat rayon
      этот район

What street number is this?
kakoy etat nomyer?
Какой этот номер?

Some Useful Words

address
adryes
адрес

arrival
pribitiye   прибытие

behind
za   за

bicycle
vyelasipyet   велосипед

departure
atyezt   отъезд

early
rana   рано

economy (ticket) – plane
turistskiy klas   туристский класс

economy (ticket) – train
f kupyeynam vagonye   в купейном вагоне

1st class (ticket) – plane
pyerviy klas   первый класс

1st class (ticket) – train
v myakhkam vagonye   в мягком вагоне

next to
ryadam s   рядом с

opposite
naprotif   напротив

seat
myesta   место

stop
astanofka   остановка

ticket
bilyet   билет

timetable
raspisaniye   расписание

Accommodation

As you probably know, it has always been quite difficult travelling with any sort of flexible itinerary: all accommodation is generally organised by a travel agent and Intourist, which is also expensive! However, there is talk in the Russian press of Intourist losing its monopoly. This section should be useful for all queries and problems to do with the accommodation you have already chosen.

Finding Accommodation

Where is a ... (around here)?

gdye (zdyes') ...?	Где (здесь) ...?
boarding house	
pansion	пансион
hotel	
gastinitsa	гостиница
tourist bureau	
byuro turizma	бюро туризма
youth hostel	
maladyozhnaya	молодёжная
turbaza	турбаза

66

I'd like a hotel ...
ya ishu gastinitsu ...   Я ищу гостиницу ...
  as cheap as possible
    kak mozhna   как можно
    dyeshevlye   дешевле
  near the centre of town
    bliska at tsentra   близко от центра
    gorada   города
  that's not too expensive
    nye slishkam   не слишком
    daraguyu   дорогую

Can I stay at a ...?
mozhna astanavit'sa   Можно остановиться
v ...?   в ...?
  cooperative hotel
    kapyerativnay   кооперативной
    gastinitse   гостинице
  private flat
    chasnay kvartirye частной квартире

How much does a room cost
(per day)?
  skol'ka stoit nomyer Сколько стоит номер
  (f sutki)?   (в сутки)?
What is included?
  shto fklyuchyeno?   Что включено?
Are there any cheaper rooms?
  yest' nomyeri   Есть номеры
  padyeshevlye?   подешевле?

Is there a reduction for children?
>*yest' skitka dlya dyetyey?*
>Есть скидка для детей?

I'd like to reserve a room.
>*ya khachu zakazat' nomyer*
>Я хочу заказать номер.

Can you please write down ...?
>*zapishitye, pazhalsta, ...*
>Запишите, пожалуйста, ...

>>the address
>>*adryes*
>>адрес
>>the price
>>*tsenu*
>>цену

Checking In

When you first arrive at a hotel you need to fill out a registration form (in English!) and leave your passport at the desk. There is almost always someone who can speak English, certainly at the Intourist desk in larger hotels.

Here is my passport.
 *vot moy **paspart***   Вот мой паспорт.
I have a reservation.
 dlya myenya uzhe   Для меня уже
 zabraniravali nomyer   забронировали номер.

I need a room for ...
 *mnye **nuzhen***   Мне нужен
 ***nomyer** dlya ...*   номер для ...
   myself
    syebya   себя
   two people
    dvaikh   двоих
   one night
    tol'ka sutki   только сутки
   two nights
    dvoye sutak   двое суток

In the room, is there ...?
 *yest' v **nomyerye** ...?*   Есть в номере ...?
Where is the room?
 *gdye **nomyer**?*   Где номер?
Can I see the room?
 mozhna pasmatryet'   Можно посмотреть
 *etat **nomyer**?*   этот номер?
Fine, I'll take it.
 kharasho, snimu   Хорошо, сниму.
Is there another room?
 *yest' **drugoy nomyer**?*   Есть другой номер?

Thanks anyway, but it's not
suitable.
> *spasiba, no eta nye*
> *padaydyot*

Спасибо, но это
не подойдёт.

Where is ...?
> *gdye ...?*

Где ...?

> hot water
> > *garyachnaya vada?*

> горячая вода

> a shower
> > *dush*

> душ

> a telephone
> > *tyelyefon*

> телефон

> a TV
> > *tyelyevizar*

> телевизор

> a toilet
> > *tualyet*

> туалет

Is there somewhere to wash
clothes?
> *mozhna gdyenibud'*
> *pachistit' adyezhdu?*

Можно где-нибудь
почистить одежду?

When will there be hot water?
> *kagda budyet*
> *garyachaya vada?*

Когда будет
горячая вода?

Is there a safe where I can
leave my valuables?
> *mozhna astavit' svai*
> *tsenasti u*
> *vas f syeyfye?*

Можно оставить
свои ценности у
вас в сейфе?

Can I please have ...?
  daytye,
  pazhalsta, ...   Дайте,
                                         пожалуйста, ...
    the bill
      shot   счёт
    the (spare) key
      (zapasnoy) klyuch   (запасной) ключ
    my passport
      *moy **paspart***   мой паспорт

Checking Out

I'm checking out ...
  ya uyezhayu ...   Я уезжаю ...
    now
      syeychas   сейчас
    midday
      f poldyen'   в полдень
    tomorrow
      zaftra   завтра

Can you please get me a taxi?
  vizavitye, pazhalsta,   Вызовите,
  taksi   пожалуйста, такси.

Requests & Complaints

Bell (for service)
   zvanok　　　　　　　　ЗВОНОК

Excuse me, something's the matter.
   izvinitye, pazhalsta,
   shto-ta nye f paryatkye　Извините, пожалуйста,
　　　　　　　　　　　　что-то не в пордке.

I have a request.
   u mye nya yest'
   proz'ba　　　　　　　У меня есть
　　　　　　　　　　　　просьба.

I can't open/close the (door/window).
   ya nye magu atkrivat'/
   zakrivat'　　　　　　Я не могу открывать/
   (dvyer'/akno)　　　　закрывать
　　　　　　　　　　　　(дверь/окно).

The toilet won't flush.
   slivnoy bachok
   isportilsa　　　　　　Сливной бачок
　　　　　　　　　　　　испортился.

It's too (hot/cold/noisy).
   slishkam (zharka/
   kholadna/shumna)　　Слишком (жарко/
　　　　　　　　　　　　холодно/шумно).

It smells.
   plokha pakhnyet — Плохо пахнет.
There are insects/mice.
   yest' nasyekomiye/
   mishi — Есть насекомые/
   мыши.
The ... doesn't work.
   ... nye ra**bo**tayet — ... не работает.
Do you have (a) ...?
   u vas yest' ...? — У вас есть ...?

Some Useful Words

air-conditioning
   kanditsia**nyer** — кондиционер
basin
   tas — таз
blanket
   ad**yeya**la — одеяло
cot
   dyetskaya kravatka — детская кроватка
cupboard
   shkaf — шкаф
curtain
   zan**avyeska** — занавеска
dirty
   gryazniy — грязный
electricity
   elye**krichyestva** — электричество
excluded
   isklyu**chyeno** — исключено

heating
   ataplyeniye   отопление
hot water
   garyachaya vada   горячая вода
included
   fklyuchyeno   включено
lift (elevator)
   lift   лифт

light
   svyet   свет
lock
   zamok   замок
mattress
   matrats   матрац
pillow
   padushka   подушка
pillowcase
   navalachka   наволочка
plug
   propka   пробка

sheet
   prastinya   простыня
shower
   dush   душ
soap
   mila   мыло
tap (faucet)
   kran   кран
TV
   tyelyevizar   телевизор
toilet
   tualyet   туалет
toilet paper
   tualyetnaya bumaga   туалетная бумага
towel
   palatyentse   полотенце
window
   akno   окно

Laundry

Is there a laundry nearby?
gdye zdyes'
prachechnaya?

Где здесь
прачечная?

Can you please ... this?
pazhalsta, vi nye
mozhetye ... eta?

Пожалуйста,
вы не можете ... это?

Where can I ... this?
gdye mozhna ... eta?

Где можно ... это?

clean
pachistit'

почистить

iron
vigladit'

быгладить

mend
pachinit'

починить

wash
pastirat'

постирать

I need it ...
nuzhna ...

Нужно ...

today
syevodnya

сегодня

tomorrow
zaftra

завтра

as soon as possible
kak mozhna skaryeye

как можно скорее

This isn't mine.
eta nye mayo

Это не моё.

Around Town

Addresses

Russian addresses are written the reverse way round to the way English-speakers are accustomed. The city and postcode come first, followed by the street, then the number, then the person's name:

г. Ленинград 103829
ул. Некрасова
д.33, корп.2, кв.15
ИВАНОВУ И.И.

In the first line, the letter г. stands for the Russian word for 'city'. Looking up the alphabet you'll be able to figure out what the next word is: Leningrad.

The next line starts with ул. which is short for 'street', улица, *ulitsa*. Other possible words used in street names include:

boulevard
   bul'var   бул. (бульвар)
lane
   pyeryeulak   пер. (переулок)
square
   ploshat'   пл. (площадь)
avenue
   praspyekt   пр. (проспект)

The third line looks confusing, but it's not really! The letter д.
stands for *dom*, ДОМ which dictionaries normally tell you means
'house', but in fact usually refers to either an apartment block or
a whole housing complex. The word корп. – *korpus*, корпус,
means one building within a complex. Then кв. – *kvartira*,
квартира, is the actual apartment.

You may have difficulties finding addresses; often streets are
not named, and maps can be hard to get. You can ask for
information at a *spravachnaye byuro*, СПРАВОЧНОЕ БЮРО.
It might be helpful to ask which metro station a certain street is
near, and once you get off the metro ask passers-by for directions
(See the Getting Around chapter). Or catch a taxi!

At the Post Office

Post Office
    pochta   ПОЧТА
Main Post Office
    glavpachtamt   ГЛАВПОЧТАМТ
Book Post
    bandyeroli   БАНДЕРОЛИ

Note that you can only send parcels overseas from main post-offices. Sending books is easy – just take them unwrapped to the book post counter, and they will wrap them and send them for you. However, all other things you have to wrap yourself and you will need to fill out customs forms – make sure you know the weight and value of each item. Mail to and from overseas can be very slow.

Please give me ...
   daytye, pazhalsta, ...   Дайте, пожалуйста, ...
      an airmail letter
         aviapis'mo   авиаписьмо
      a stamp (for this)
         marku (dlya etava)   марку (для этого)
      a postcard
         atkritku   открытку

I'd like to send this/these ...
   ya khachu paslat' eta ... Я хочу послать это ...
      by airmail
         aviapochtay   авиапочтой
      express
         snarochnim   с нарочным
      by registered mail
         zakaznim   заказным

I'd like to send a telegram.
   ya khachu paslat'   Я хочу послать
   tyelyegramu   телеграмму.
How much will that be?
   skol'ka stoit?   Сколько стоит?

I'm expecting ...
ya zhdu ...   Я жду ...
   a letter
    pis'mo   письмо
   a parcel
    pasilku   посылку

Here is my passport.
   vot moy paspart   Вот мой паспорт.

Telephone

Local and international calls are relatively cheap. You can book international calls at your hotel, but it is quite straightforward to go to a telegraph office, *tyelyegraf*, ТЕЛЕГРАФ, with the number and place written down; they will ring the number for you and call you to a booth.

I'd like to book a call to ...
(for ... minutes).
   ya khachu zakazat'   Я хочу заказать
   tyelyefoniy razgavor   телефонный разговор
   s ... (na ... minut).   с ... (на ... минут).
How much will it cost?
   skol'ka eta   Сколько это
   budyet stoit'?   будет стоить?
We were cut off.
   nas razyedinili   Нас разъединили.
I got the wrong number.
   vi myenya sayedinili   Вы меня соединили
   nyepravil'na   неправильно.

At the Bank

Currency Exchange
   abmyen valyuti   ОБМЕН ВАЛЮТЫ

Bank
   bank   БАНК

You will already know how valuable foreign (hard) currency is in the Soviet Union. Special tourist shops called 'Beriozka', *byeryoska,* Берёзка, and certain other shops and restaurants only accept foreign currency, but they are generally much better supplied than rouble shops. People on the street may offer to change your money at a good rate but this is illegal – and since you have to declare how much foreign currency you have as you enter and leave the USSR, with receipts for any money spent or exchanged, it is risky.

I'd like to change ...
   ya khachu
   abmyenyat' ...   Я хочу обменять ...
      this into roubles
         eta na rubli   это на рубли
      a travellers' cheque
         darozhniy chyek   дорожный чек
      (100) dollars/pounds/
      deutschmarks
         (sto) dolarav/   (сто) долларов/
         funtav/marak   фунтов/марок

What is the exchange rate?
   kakoy kurs?   Какой курс?

What is your commission?
*skol'ka vi byeryotye
za abmyen?*

Сколько вы берёте
за обмен?

Please write it down.
*zapishitye eta,
pazhalsta*

Запишите это,
пожалуйста.

Do you accept this credit card/
foreign currency?
*vi prinimayetye etu
kryeditnuyu kartachku/
valyutu?*

Вы принимаете эту
кредитную
карточку/валюту?

Can I have money transferred
to here?
*mozhna paluchit'
zdyes' dyen'gi
pa pyeryevodu?*

Можно получить
здесь деньги
по переводу?

How long will it take?
*skol'ka nuzhna
vryemyeni?*

Сколько нужно
времени?

Have you received my money
yet?
*vi paluchili mai
dyen'gi?*

Вы получили мои
деньги?

Sightseeing

I'd like to see (a/the) ...

ya khachu pasmatryet' ...   Я хочу посмотреть ...

cemetery
kladbishye   кладбище

church
tserkaf'   церковь

(Tretyakov) Gallery
(tryet'yakofskuyu)   (Третьковскую)
galyeryeyu   Галерею

Hermitage
ermitash   Эрмитаж

Kremlin
kreml'   Кремль

Lenin's Mausoleum
mavzalyey lyenina   Мавзолей Ленина

memorial
pamyatnik   памятник

mosque
myechyet'   мечеть

museum
muzyey   музей

palace
dvaryets   дворец

Red Square
krasnuyu ploshat'   Красную площадь

synagogue
sinagogu   синагогу

university
univyersityet   университет

What do you recommend
seeing?
   shto vi savyetuyetye
   pasmatryet'?   Что вы советуете
                  посмотреть?

I'm/We're interested in ...
   ya intyeryesuyus'/
   mi intyeryesuyemsa ...   Я интересуюсь/
                  Мы интересуемся ...
    architecture
      arkhityekturay   архитектурой
    art
      iskustvam   искусством
    churches
      tserkvami   церквами
    handicrafts
      ryemyoslami   ремёслами
    history
      istoriyey   историей
    icons
      ikonami   иконами
    literature
      lityeraturay   литературой
    sculpture
      skul'pturay   скульптурой

Is there a discount for
students/children?
   yest' skitka dlya
   studyentav/dyetyey?   Есть скидка для
                  студентов/детей?

Do you have ... ?
  u vas yest' ...?　　У вас есть ...?
    a catalogue (in English)
      katalok (na　　каталог (на
      angliyskam　　английском
      yazikye)　　языке)
    postcards
      atkritki　　открытки
    slides
      slaydi　　слайды
    souvenirs
      suvyeniri　　сувениры

Some Useful Words
ancient
  dryevniy　　древний
archaeological
  arkhyealagicheskiy　　археологический
market
  rinak　　рынок
monument
  pamyatnik　　памтник
old city
  dryevniy gorat　　древний город
ruins
  razvalini　　развалины

No Cameras!
  fotagrafiravat'　　ФОТОГРАФИРОВАТЬ
  vaspryeshayetsa!　　ВОСПРЕЩАЕТСЯ!

Signs

A big part of culture shock is when things look similar to what you're used to – as in any big city – but all the writing is in another alphabet! You'll find more specific signs in other sections (like names of shops under 'Shopping') but here is a list of common signs you'll find everywhere.

Cashier	
kassa	КАССА
Caution	
astarozhna	ОСТОРОЖНО
Caution	
byeryegis'	БУФЕТ
Closed	
zakrita	ЗАКРЫТО
Entrance	
fkhod	ВХОД
Entry Prohibited	
fkhod vaspryeshyon	ВХОД ВОСПРЕЩЕН
Exit	
vikhad	ВЫХОД
Gents	
mushskoy tualyet	М / МУЖСКОЙ ТУ АЛЕТ
Information	
sprafki	СПРАВКИ
Information desk	
spravachnaye byuro	СПРАВОЧНОЕ БЮРО
Intourist	
inturist	ИНТУРИСТ

Ladies
zhenskiy tualyet
Ж / ЖЕНСКИЙ ТУАЛЕТ

Lift (Elevator)
lift
ЛИФТ

Lost Property Office
byuro nakhodak
БЮРО НАХОДОК

Metro/Underground
myetro
М / МЕТРО

No Entry
fkhoda nyet
ВХОДА НЕТ

No Exit
vikhada nyet
ВЫХОДА НЕТ

No Seats (Sold Out)
myest nyet
МЕСТ НЕТ

No Smoking
nye kurit'
НЕ КУРИТЬ

Out of Order
nye rabotayet
НЕ РАБОТАЕТ

Prohibited
zapryeshayetsa
ЗАПРЕЩАЕТСЯ

Pull
syebye/tyanitye
К СЕБЕ/ТЯНИТЕП

Push
at syebya/talkaytye
ОТ СЕБЯ/ТОЛКАЙТЕ

Refreshments
bufyet
БУФЕТ

Reserved/Engaged
zanyata
ЗАНЯТО

Sale
raspradazha
РАСПРОДАЖА

Taxi	
taksi	Т/ТАКСИ
Telephone	
tyelyefon	ТЕЛЕФО
Toilets	
tualyet	ТУАЛЕТ
Traffic Police	ГАИ (abbreviation)
Under Repair	
ryemont	РЕМОНТ
Vacant	
svabodna	СВОБОДНО
Way to ...	
pyeryekhod v/na ...	ПЕРЕХОД В/НА

Entertainment

Soviet entertainment had a reputation of being dull, but now there is a kind of cultural catharsis, with an extremely lively theatre, cinema and art scene. Newly opened cooperatives offer all types of entertainment. Soft porn and strip shows are popular with Russian men, so there's 'progress' for you. Gay venues are illegal. Some new restaurants have an intimate atmosphere, but often Russians go to restaurants in groups, where a whole evening of food, drink and dancing is provided.

Cinema	
kino	КИНО
Restaurant	
ryestaran	РЕСТОРАН

Bar
  bar БАР
Disco
  diskatyeka ДИСКОТЕКА

I want to go ...
  ya khachu payti ... Я хочу пойти ...
    to a bar
      v bar в бар
    to the cinema
      f kino в кино
    to a concert
      na kantsert на концерт
    dancing
      patantsevat' потанцевать
    to a disco
      v diskatyeku в дискотеку
    to a nightclub
      v nachnoy klub в ночной клуб
    to see a show
      pasmatryet' посмотреть
      spyektakl' спектакль
    to a skating rink
      na katok на каток
    to the theatre
      f tyeatr в театр
    for a walk
      pagulyat' погулять
    to the zoo
      zaapark в зоопарк

Where is the ticket office?
  gdye kassa?   Где касса?
How much is a ticket?
  skol'ka stoit bilyet?   Сколько стоит билет?

What's on?
  shto idyot?   Что идёт?
One ticket/Two tickets please.
  adin bilyet/dva bilyeta,   Один билет/два билета,
  pazhalsta   пожалуйста.

In the Country

Weather

It's ...

(too) cold	**(slishkam) kholadna**	(Слишком) холодно.
cool	**prakhladna**	Прохладно.
hot	**zharka**	Жарко.
humid	**dushna**	Душно.
raining	**idyot dozhd'**	Идёт дождь.
snowing	**idyot snyeg**	Идёт снег.
warm	**tyeplo**	Тепло.
windy	**vyetryena**	Ветрено.

91

Some Useful Phrases

What's the weather like
today?

*kakaya syevodnya
pagoda?*

Какая сегодня
погода?

Will it be cold/warm?

*budyet kholadna/
tyeplo?*

Будет холодно/
тепло?

Will it rain?

budyet dozht'?

Будет дождь?

Will it snow?

budyet snyek?

Будет снег?

Some Useful Words

ice

lyot

лёд

slippery

skol'skiy

скольский

slush

slyakat'

слякоть

snow

snyek

снег

Seasons

spring
   vyesna   весна
summer
   lyeta   лето
autumn
   osyen'   осень
winter
   zima   зима

Sights

I would like to see ..
   ya ochyen'
   khatyela (f)/*khatyel* (m)
   bi pasmatryet'
   Я очень хотела (f)/ хотел (m) бы посмотреть ...

We would very much like to see ...
   mi ochyen' khatyeli
   bi pasmatryet'
   Мы очень хотели бы посмотреть ...

   a beach
     plyash   пляж
   a collective farm
     kalkhos   колхоз
   a factory
     fabriku   фабрику
   a forest
     lyes   лес
   the harbour
     gavan'   гавань
   the lake
     ozyera   озеро

mountains
   gori   горы
the river
   ryeku   реку
the sea
   morye   море
a state farm
   savkhos   совхоз

How long will it take to get
there?
   skol'ka nuzhna vryemyeni Сколько нужно времени
   papast' tuda?   попасть туда?
Can we walk?
   mozhna itti pyeshkom? Можно идти пешком?

Animals, Birds & Insects
Are there ... around here?
   fstryechayesh' zdyes' ...? Встречаешь здесь ...?
Do you have ...?
   u vas nyet ...?   У вас нет ...?
   bears
      myedvyed'yef   медведьев
   birds
      ptits   птиц
   cats
      koshek   кошек
   chickens
      kur   кур
   cows
      karof   коров

dogs	
sabak	собак
fish	
rip	рыб
flies	
mukh	мух
horses	
lashadyey	лошадей
mosquitoes	
maskitaf	москитов
pigs	
svinyey	свиней
rats	
kris	крыс
sheep	
avyets	овец
spiders	
paukof	пауков
wild animals	
zvyeryeh	зверей
wolves	
valkof	волков

Camping

Where is a/the camping
ground?
   gdye kemping?   Где кемпинг?
Can we put up a tent here?
   mozhna pastavit'   Можно поставить
   palatku zdyes'?   палатку здесь?

Where is the administration?
 gdye administratsiya?   Где администрация?
Can we hire a boat/a tent?
 mozhna vzyat' naprakat'   Можно взять напрокат
 lotku/palatku?   лодку /палатку ?

Some Useful Words

camping ground
 kemping   кемпинг
farm
 fyerma   ферма
field
 polye   поле
food
 yeda   еда
matches
 spichki   спички
saucepan
 kastryulya   кастрюл
shower
 dush   душ
tent
 palatka   палатка
toilet
 tualyet   туалет
tree
 dyeryeva   дерево
(drinking) water
 (pit' yevaya) vada   питьевая вода

Food

Russians have a different tradition of eating out – they tend to see it as a whole evening's entertainment, with multiple courses, music and dancing. Service is generally very slow but this is partly because there is no rush to finish. Western restaurants can seem very restrained in comparison.

Russians toast before each round (usually then downing vodka followed by a bite of something). 'To your health!' is *za vashe zdarov'ye!*, За ваше здоровь! It is also polite to say before eating 'Bon appetit!', *priyatnava apyetita!*, Притного апетита!

Restaurants

It is generally impossible to get into a decent restaurant without booking, but it is also difficult to book, especially by telephone. The best strategy seems to be going to the restaurant the day before or that morning, and speaking personally to the manager, *administratar*, администратор.

Where can I get a quick snack?

gdye mozhna bistra pyeryekusit'?

Где можно быстро перекусить?

Is there a good restaurant around here?

yest' zdyes' kharoshiy ryestaran?

Есть здесь хороший ресторан?

Where is a ...?
  gdye yest' ...?   Где есть ...?
    bar
      bar   БАР
    cafe (generally you have
    to order a meal)
      kafeh   КАФЕ
    cafeteria (very basic, no
    alcohol)
      stalovaya   СТОЛОВАЯ
    coffee shop
      kafeh-kandityerskaya   КАФЕ-
                           КОНДИТЕРСКАЯ
    ice-cream cafe
      kafeh-marozhenaye   КАФЕ-МОРОЖЕНОЕ
    restaurant (most up-
    market)
      ryestaran   РЕСТОРАН
    snack bar
      bufyet/   БУФЕТ/
      zakusachnaya   ЗАКУСОЧНАЯ

Booked Out
  myest nyet   МЕСТ НЕТ
Reserved
  stol zakazan   СТОЛ ЗАКАЗАН

My surname is (Simmons).
  maya familiya –   Моя фамилия –
  (simans)   (Симмонс).
I'm by myself.
  ya adna (f)/*adin* (m)   Я одна (f)/один (m).

I need a table for ... people.
  mnye nuzhen stolik na ...   Мне нужен столик на ...
    two
      dvaikh   двоих
    three
      traikh   троих

breakfast
  zaftrak   завтрак
lunch
  abyet   обед
dinner (evening meal)
  uzhin   ужин

Tonight at (nine o'clock).
  syevodnya vyecheram v   Сегодня вечером в
  (dyevyat' chyasof)   девять часов.
I have booked.
  ya uzhe zakazala (f)/   Я уже заказала (f)/
  zakazal (m) *stolik*   заказал (m) столик.

Should we wait?
  nam padazhdat'?   Нам подождать?

Ordering & Paying

Can I have a menu please?
  daytye, pazhalsta,   Дайте, пожалуйста,
  myenyu   меню.
Do you have a fixed menu?
  u vas komplyeksniy   У вас комплексный
  abyet?   обед?
How much is it/this?
  skol'ka eta stoit?   Сколько это стоит?
Is (this) available?
  (eta) yest'?   (Это) есть?
What is this?
  shto eta?   Что это?

I'd like ...
  ya vaz'mu ...   Я возьму ...
We'd like ...
  mi vaz'myom ...   Мы возьмём ...

Please bring ...
   prinyesitye, ...   Принесите,
   pazhalsta,   пожалуйста, ...

      an ashtray
         pyepyel'nitsu   пепельницу
      another bottle
         yesho adnu butilku   ещё одну бутылку
      a fork
         vilku   вилку
      a (wine) glass
         ryumku   рюмку
      a glass of water
         stakan vodi   стакан воды
      a knife
         nosh   нож
      a napkin
         salfyetku   салфетку
      a spoon
         loshku   ложку

This dish is cold/inedible.
   blyuda khalodnaye/   Блюдо холодное/
   nyesyedobnaye   несъедобное.
We've been waiting ages.
   mi uzhe davno zhdyom Мы уже давно ждём.
Nothing else, thank you.
   spasiba, bol'she   Спасибо, больше
   nichyevo   ничего.
That was all delicious.
   fsyo bila ochyen'   Всё было очень
   fkusna   вкусно.

Could we have the bill please?
   daytye, pazhalsta, shot   Дайте, пожалуйста,
                              счёт.

Do you take credit cards/
foreign currency?
   vi byeryotye kryeditniye   Вы берёте кредитные
   kartachki/inastranuyu   карточки/иностранн-
   valyutu?   ую валюту?

Hors d'Oeuvres

caviar (red/black)
   ikra (krasnaya/   икра (красная/
   chyornaya)   чёрная)
diced vegetable salad
   vinyegryet   винегрет

eggs
   yaytsa   яйца
     pickled
       marinovaniye   маринованные
     with onions
       slukam   с луком
     with sour cream
       sa smyetanay/   со сметаной/
       f smyetanye   в сметане
     in vinegar
       suksusam   с уксусом

gherkins
   agurtsi   огурцы

herrings
  syelyotka   селёдка
mushrooms
  gribi   грибы
pate
  pashtyet   паштет
salad
  salat   салат
sprats (like sardines)
  shproti   шпроты

Soup

beetroot (normally with meat)
  borsh   борщ
broth
  bul'yon   бульон
cold
  akroshka   окрошка
cucumber & kidney
  rassol'nik   рассольник
fish
  ukha   уха
thick cabbage
  shyi   щи

heavily seasoned (normally
with meat)
   salyanka   солянка
   creamed
     sup pyurey   суп-пюре
   with noodles
     vyermishelyeviy   вермишелевый
   with meat
     myasnoy   мясной
   with fish
     ribniy   рыбный
   with meatballs
     s frikadyel'kami   с рикадельками
   with an egg
     syaytsom   с яйцом

Meat & Fish Dishes

Good quality meat is not easy to get. However, Russian cooking
tends to centre around meat.

beef
   gavyadina   говядина
beef stroganoff
   byefstroganaf   бефстроганов
chicken
   kuritsa   курица
chicken Kiev
   katlyeti pakiyefski   котлеты по-киевски
cod
   tryeska   треска

fillet
  filyeh   филе
fish
  riba   рыба
garlic sausage
  kupati   купаты
goulash
  gulyash   гуляш
kebab
  kyebap   кебаб
lamb
  baranina   баранина
meatballs
  bitochki   биточки
pork
  svinina   свинина
rabbit
  krolik   кролик
rissoles
  katlyeti   котлеты
salmon
  syomga   сёмга
sausages
  sasiski   сосиски
schnitzel
  shnitsel'   шницель

shaslik
   shashlik   шашлык
steak
   bifshteks   бифштекс
stew
   ragu   рагу
tongue
   yazik   язык
veal
   tyelyatina   телятина

Fruit & Vegetables

It takes some patience being a vegetarian, or even not particularly liking meat, in the Soviet Union. Vegetables are generally seen as an accompaniment, and they can be hard to get, or just very expensive, as they are at the private markets. The Istra Potato Cafe in Moscow has been known to run out of potatoes. Preserved vegetables, such as pickles, are very common.

I'm a vegetarian.
   ya vyegyetarianka (f)/   Я вегетарианка (f)/
   vyegyetarianyets (m)   вегетарианец (m).
I'm on a strict diet.
   ya sablyudayu   Я соблюдаю строгую
   stroguyu diyetu   диету.
I don't eat meat.
   ya nye yem myasnova   Я не ем мясного.
I don't eat dairy products.
   ya nye yem malochnava Я не ем молочного.

Fruit

apples
yablaki   яблоки

berries
yagada   ягода

grapes
vinagrat   виноград

lemon
limon   лимон

oranges
apyel' sini   апельсины

watermelon
arbus   арбуз

Vegetables

beetroot
svyokla   свёкла

broad beans
babi   бобы

cabbage
kapusta   капуста

carrots
markof'   морковь

chips
zharyenaya kartoshka   жареная картошка

gherkins
agurtsi   огурцы

mashed potato
kartofyel' naye pyureh   картофельное пюре

mushrooms
gribi   грибы

onions
  luk   лук
peas
  garokh   горох
potatoes
  kartofyel'   картофель
tomatoes
  pamidori   помидоры

Dairy Products
butter
  masla   масло
cheese
  sir   сыр
cottage cheese
  tvarok   творог
cream
  slifki   сливки
ice cream
  marozhenaye   мороженое
sour cream
  smyetana   сметана

Other Food & Condiments
baked cheese cake (delicious!)
  zapyekanka   запеканка творожная
  tvorazhnaya
biscuits
  pyechyen'ye   печенье

bread (white/black)
   khlyeb   хлеб
   (byeliy/chyorniy) (белый/чёрный)
cabbage rolls
   galuptsi   голубцы
cake
   tort   торт
cake (small)
   prozhnaye   пирожное
cereal (groats)
   kasha   каша
dumplings (large meat or
cabbage)
   pirashki   пирожки
dumplings (small boiled meat)
   pyel' myeni   пельмени
egg
   yaytso   яйцо
fried egg
   yaichnitsa   яичница
jam
   varyen' ye   варенье
mustard
   garchitsa   горчица
omelette
   amlyet   омлет
open sandwich
   butyerbrot   бутерброд
pancakes (small)
   blinchiki   блинчики

pancakes (buckwheat)
  blini   блины

pasta
  makaroni   макароны

pepper
  pyeryets   перец

pilaf (rice dish, usually with meat)
  plof   плов

pudding (baked)
  zapyekanka   запеканка

rice
  ris   рис

rolls
  bulachki   булочки

salt
  sol'   соль

sauce
  sous   соус

stewed fruit (sometimes a drink)
  kampot   компот

sugar
  sakhar   сахар

waffles
  vafli   вафли

Methods of Cooking

baked
   zapyechoniy   запечённый

boiled
   varyoniy   варёный

fried
   zharyeniy   жареный

grilled
   zharyeniy na   жареный на
   rashpyerye   рашпере

stuffed
   farshirovaniy   фаршированный

in tomato sauce
   f tamatye   в томате

with apples
   syablakami   с блоками

with cabbage
   skapustay   с капустой

with meat
   smyasam   с мясом

with onions
   slukam   с луком

Drinks

Milk with tea and coffee is quite rare. Some Soviet wines and
spirits can be very good, especially those from Georgia. Cognac
is almost as popular as vodka. As in other parts of Europe, beer
and wine are normally not chilled. Fruit juices can be harder to get
than alcohol – be prepared to get a vodka and orange that is a glass
of vodka with a bit of orange juice poured on top.

Could you please chill this?
  akhladitye eta,   Охладите это,
  pazhalsta   пожалуйста.
coffee
  kofi   кофе
fruit juice
  sok   сок
hot chocolate
  kakao   какао
kvass (cold drink made from
bread and yeast)
  kvas   квас
milk
  malako   молоко
milk shake
  malochniy kakteyl   молочный коктейл
mineral water
  minyeral'naya vada минеральная вода
Russian lemonade
  limanat   лимонад
soda water
  gazirovannaya vada газированная вода
starchy drink
  kisyel'   кисель
water
  vada   вода
tea
  chay   чай
thick sour milk
  kyefir   кефир

Turkish coffee
kofi pavastochnamu   кофе по-восточному

Extras
with ice
sal'dom   со льдом
with lemon
slimonam   с лимоном
with milk
smalakom   с молоком
with sugar
s sakharam   с сахаром

Alcoholic Drinks
beer
piva   пиво
champagne
shampanskaye   шампанское
cocktail
kakteyl   коктейль
cognac
kan'yak   коньяк
liqueur
likyor   ликёр
wine (white/red/dry/sweet)
vino (byelaye/krasnaye/   вино (белое/красное/
sukhoye/slatkaye)   сухое/сладкое)
whisky
viski   виски
vodka
votka   водка

Shopping

Supply in shops may be quite unpredictable and at times rationing has even been introduced in Moscow and Leningrad. However, staples such as bread and milk are not rationed and are generally available. There are some private shops called 'cooperatives' and private markets which may be well stocked but are comparatively expensive.

Many tourists only come into contact with the state-run tourist shops called 'Beriozkas', *byeryoska*, Берёзка. They are well stocked with a wide range of goods including souvenirs, postage stamps, and luxury goods such as vodka and chocolates. However, they only accept foreign currency, so Russians in effect can't shop there. On the other hand, you will not be able to buy rationed goods in normal shops! Beriozkas accept credit cards, and if you pay with travellers' cheques, you will be given change in hard currency.

Shops are normally open six days a week; the day they are closed is often not Sunday, but a weekday, which is written on the front. There may be an hour-long lunch break. Food shops generally stay open seven days a week until 9 pm.

Business Hours
from ... to ...
   atkrita/magazin   ОТКРЫТО/МАГАЗИН
   rabotayet s ... do ...   РАБОТАЕТ С ... ДО ...

Closed for Lunch
from ... to ...
   pyeryeriv na abyed s ... ПЕРЕРЫВ НА ОБЕД С
   do ...   ... ДО ...

Closed Tuesdays
   vikhadnoy dyen' :   ВЫХОДНОЙ ДЕНЬ:
   ftornik   ВТОРНИК

Self-Service
   sama-apsluzhivaniye   САМООБСЛУЖИВАНИЕ

Finding Shops

An alternative in inverted commas indicates what might actually be written above the shop, eg 'Books' as opposed to Bookshop.

Where is a ...

gdye ...?		Где ...?
bookshop		
	knizhniy	КНИЖНЫЙ
	magazin	МАГАЗИН 'КНИГИ'
bookshop (second-hand)		
	bukhinist	БУКИНИСТ
bottle shop		
	viniy magazin	ВИННЫЙ МАГАЗИН 'ВИНО'
bread shop		
	bulashnaya	БУЛОЧНАЯ
camera shop		
	fotamagazin	ФОТОМАГАЗИН
clothing shop		
	magazin	МАГАЗИН
	adyezhdi	ОДЕЖДЫ
children's clothing shop		
	dyetskaya adyezhda	ДЕТСКАЯ ОДЕЖДА
men's clothing shop		
	mushskaya	МУЖСКАЯ
	adyezhda	ОДЕЖДА
women's clothing shop		
	zhenskaya adyezhda	ЖЕНСКАЯ ОДЕЖДА
department store		
	univyermak	УНИВЕРМАГ

dry-cleaner's
  khimchistka   ХИМЧИСТКА
electrical shop
  elyektratavari   ЭЛЕКТРОТОВАРЫ
florist
  tsvyetochniy   ЦВЕТОЧНЫЙ
  magazin   МАГАЗИН 'ЦВЕТЫ'
food shop
  gastranom   ГАСТРОНОМ
haberdashery
  galantyeryeya   ГАЛАНТЕРЕЯ
hairdresser
  parikmakherskaya   ПАРИКМАХЕРСКАЯ
hardware
  khazyaystvyeniy   ХОЗЯЙСТВЕННЫЙ
  magazin   МАГАЗИН
                                 'ИНСТРУМЕНТЫ'
jeweller's
  yuvyelirniy magazin   ЮВЕЛИРНЫЙ
                                 МАГАЗИН
laundry
  prachyechnaya   ПРАЧЕЧНАЯ
market
  rinak   РЫНОК
second-hand (usually
clothing) shop
  kamissioniy magazin   КОМИССИОННЫЙ
                                 МАГАЗИН
newspaper stand
  gazyetniy kiosk   ГАЗЕТНЫЙ КИОСК
                                 'СОЮЗПЕЧАТЬ'

pharmacy
 aptyeka   АПТЕКА
shoe shop
 magazin obuvi   МАГАЗИН ОБУВИ
                             'ОБУВЬ'
shop(s)
 magazin(i)   МАГАЗИН(Ы)
souvenir shop
 magazin suvyeniraf   МАГАЗИН
                             СУВЕНИРОВ
                             'СУВЕНИРЫ'
sports shop
 sport tavari   СПОРТТОВАРЫ
State record label
 myelodiya   'МЕЛОДИЯ'
stationer's
 kantselyarskiye   КАНЦЕЛЯРСКИЕ
 tavari   ТОВАРЫ
supermarket
 univyersam   УНИВЕРСАМ
tobacconist
 tabachniy   ТАБАЧНЫЙ
 magazin   МАГАЗИН
                             'ТАБАК'
toy shop
 magazin igrushek   МАГАЗИН
                             ИГРУШЕК

Making a Purchase

Often shops have a cashier at a separate desk, where you have to pay, and then take the receipt to pick up what you have chosen.

I'd like to buy ...
ya khachu kupit' ...   Я хочу купить ...

Could you please show me ...
pakazhitye, pazhalsta, ...   Покажите,
                                 пожалуйста, ...

     one of those
         vot takoy   вот такой

     that
         eta   это

     half a kg
         polkilo   полкило

I'm just looking.
ya tol'ka smatryu   Я только смотрю.

How much does it cost?
skol'ka eta stoit?   Сколько это стоит?

Do you have a different one?
u vas yest' drugoy?   У вас есть другой?

I want something ...
    ya ishu koye-shto ...   Я ищу кое-что ...
    a bit cheaper
        padyeshyevlye   подешевле
    of better quality
        luchsheva kachestva   лучшего качества
    a different colour
        drugova tsvyeta   другого цвета
    bigger
        pabol'she   побольше
    smaller
        pamyen'she   поменьше

Does it have a guarantee?
    garantiya yest'?   Гарантия есть?
I'll take it.
    vaz'mu   Возьму.
That's all, thanks.
    spasiba, eta fsyo   Спасибо, это всё.
Thanks, but it's not quite what
I'm after.
    spasiba, no eta nye   Спасибо, но это не
    safsyem to, shto ya   совсем то, что я
    khachu   хочу.

How much altogether?
   skol'ka fsyevo?   Сколько всего?
Do you take credit cards?
   vi byeryotye kryeditniye   Вы берёте кредитные
   kartachki/inastranuyu   карточки/иностран-
   valyutu?   ную валюту?
Can you please wrap it?
   zavyernitye, pazhalsta?   Заверните,
                      пожалуйста?
Do you have a bag?
   u vas yest' pakyet?   У вас есть пакет?

Some Useful Words

adaptor (for this)
   pyeryekhodnuyu   переходную
   razyetku (dlya etava)   розетку (для этого)
amber
   yantar'   янтарь
bag
   myeshok   мешок
battery (for this)
   bataryeyku (dlya   батерейку (для
   etava)   этого)
bottle
   butilka   бутылка
camera
   fotaparat   фотоаппарат
candles
   svyechi   свечи

coffee
kofi кофе

handbag
sumku сумку

map
kartu карту

matches
spichki спички

plug (for this)
vilku (dlya etava) вилку (для этого)

postcard
atkritku открытку

(short-wave) radio
(karatkavolnavniy) (коротковолновный)
radiopriyomnik радиоприёмник

receipt
kvitantsiya квитанция

Russian peasant doll
matryoshku матрёшку

slides
slaydi слайды

souvenir
suvyenir сувенир

thread
nitachku ниточку

watch
chasi часы

watch strap
ryemyeshok dlya chasov ремешок для часов

Film & Photography

I'd like ... (for this camera).

  *mnye **nada** ...*
  (dlya etava fotaparata)

    a battery
      bataryeyku

    B&W film
      chyorna-byeluyu
      plyonku

    colour film
      tsvyetnuyu plyonku

    slide film
      *plyonku dlya **slaydaf***

    a video tape
      vidyeokasyetu

Can you please develop (and print) this?

  pazhalsta, prayavitye (i atpyechataytye) eta?

When will they be ready?

  kagda snimki budut gatovi?

Мне надо ... (для этого фотоаппарата).

    батарейку

    чёрно-белую
    плёнку

    цветную плёнку

    плёнку дл слайдов

    видеокассету

Пожалуйста, провите (и отпечатайте) это.

Когда снимки будут готовы?

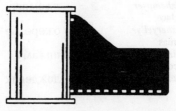

Clothing & Jewellery

I would like to buy (a) ...

ya khachu kupit' ...   Я хочу купить ...

belt
    poyas   пояс

blouse
    blusku   блузку

dress
    plat'ye   платье

earrings
    syer'gi   серьги

gloves
    pyerchatki   перчатки

handkerchief
    nasavoy platok   носовой платок

hat
    shlyapu   шляпу

jacket
    kurtku   куртку

jeans
    dzhinsi   джинсы

jumper
    dzhempyer   джемпер

necklace
    azheryel'ye   ожерелье

pyjamas
    pizhamu   пижаму

raincoat
    dazhdyevik   дождевик

ring
kal'tso кольцо
scarf
sharf шарф
shirt
rubashku рубашку
shoes
tufli туфли
skirt
yupku юбку
socks
naski носки
stockings
chulki чулки
suit
kastyum костюм
swimsuit
kupal'niy купальный
kastyum костюм
tie
galstuk галстук
trousers
bryuki брюки
T-shirt
mayku майку

It's (not) for me.
eta (nye) dlya myenya Это (не) для меня.
I don't know Russian sizes.
ya nye znayu ruskikh Я не знаю русских
razmyeraf размеров.

Can you please measure me?
*pazhalsta, snimaytye
smyenya myerku*

Пожалуйста, снимайте
с меня мерку.

Can I try it on?
mozhna primyerit'?

Можно примерить?

Where's the changing room?
gdye primyerachnaya?

Где примерочная?

Do you have a mirror?
u vas yest' zyerkala?

У вас есть зеркало?

That's fine, I'll take it.
*eta kak ras, ya eta
vaz'mu*

Это как раз, я это
возьму.

Do you have anything ...?
*u vas yest' shto-
nibut'...?*

У вас есть что-
нибудь ...?

    a bit bigger (especially
    here)
       *pabol'she
       (asobyenna zdyes')*

побольше
(особенно здесь)

    a bit smaller
       pamyen'she

поменьше

    a bit longer
       padlinyeye

подлиннее

    a bit shorter
       pakarochye

покороче

    a bit warmer
       patyeplyeye

потеплее

    a different colour
       drugova tsvyeta

другого цвета

made out of ...
   iz ...   из ...

     amber
       yantarya   янтаря

     cotton
       bumazhnay tkani   бумажной ткани

     fake fur
       iskustvennava   искусственного
       myekha   меха

     gold
       zolata   золота

     leather
       kozhi   кожи

     silver
       syeryebra   серебра

     wool
       shersti   шерсти

     with spots
       v garoshek   в горошек

     with stripes
       f palosku   в полоску

Colours

black
  chyorniy   чёрный
blue (light)
  galuboy   голубой
blue (dark)
  siniy   синний
brown
  karichnyeviy   коричневый
dark
  tyomna   тёмно

green
   zyelyoniy   зелёный
light
   svyetla   светло
orange
   aranzheviy   оранжевый
pink
   rozaviy   розовый
purple
   fialyetaviy   фиолетовый
red
   krasniy   красный
white
   byeliy   белый
yellow
   zholtiy   жёлтый

Hairdresser

Can I make an appointment
for (Tuesday)?
   mozhna zapisat'sa   Можно записаться
   na (ftornik)?   на (вторник)?
(Just) a haircut, please.
   (tol'ka) pastrigitye,   (Только) постригите,
   pazhalsta   пожалуйста.
Just a trim/neaten it up.
   pazhalsta,   Пожалуйста,
   padravnyaytye   подравните мне
   mnye volasi   волосы.

Books & Stationery

Newspapers and magazines are generally sold at newspaper stands along the footpath.

Do you have ...?
   u vas yest' ...?   У вас есть ...?
      a book about Russian art
         kniga a ruskam   книга о русском
         iskustvye   искусстве
      children's books
         dyetskiye knigi   детские книги
      a text book to learn
      Russian
         uchyebnik pa   учебник по
         ruskamu yaziku   русскому языку
      a nice book with photo-
      graphs (of this city/of this
      republic)
         kharoshiy fotoal'bom   хороший
         (etava gorada/   фотоальбом
         etay ryespubliki)   (этого города/этой
                            республики)
      a Russian cookery book
         kniga a ruskay   книга о русской
         kukhnye   кухне
      a guidebook
         putyevadityel'   путеводитель
      a map of the town
         plan gorada   план города
      a road map
         karta darok   карта дорог

a book about the USSR
  kniga a eseseser   книга о СССР
posters
  plakati   плакаты
(books) in English
  (knigi) na angliyskam   (книги) на
  yazikye   английском зыке
a (pocket) dictionary
  (karmaniy) slavar'   (карманный)
                                      словарь

(foreign) newspapers/
magazines
  (inastraniye) gazyeti/   (иностранные)
  zhurnali   газеты/журналы
Moscow News – (a very
popular radical weekly,
also printed in English)
  maskofskiye novasti   Московские
                                      новости

I need ...
  mnye nada ...   Мне надо ...
    airmail paper
      bumagu dlya   бумагу для
      aviapochti   авиапочты
    a biro
      ruchku   ручку
    envelopes
      kanvyerti   конверты
    a notebook
      blaknot   блокнот
    a pencil
      karandash   карандаш
    sellotape
      lyentu   ленту
    string
      byechyofku   бечёвку
    wrapping paper
      abyortachnuyu   обёрточную
      bumagu   бумагу
    writing paper
      pachtovuyu bumagu   почтовую бумагу

Health

You can always receive quick, good medical attention by contacting the desk or Intourist in your hotel. Medical care is free, but medication will cost some money and is sometimes very hard to get. Tampons and condoms are basically unavailable. If possible, avoid tap water; mineral water is sold everywhere.

Could you please call a
doctor?
   vizavitye vracha,   Вызовите врача,
   pazhalsta?   пожалуйста.

Where is a/the ...?
   gdye ...?   Где ...?
     chemist (pharmacy)
      aptyeka   аптека
     dentist
      zubnoy vrach   зубной врач
     doctor
      vrach   врач
     hospital
      bal'nitsa   больница

БОЛЬНИЦА

Complaints

I have ...
   u myenya ...   У меня...
She has ...
   u nyeyo ...   У неё ...
He has...
   u nyevo ...   У него ...

an allergy		
	allyergiya	аллергия
asthma		
	astma	астма
backache		
	bol' f spinye	боль з спине
a burn		
	azhok	ожог
a chill		
	prastuda	простуда
a cold		
	nasmark	насморк
constipation		
	zapor	запор
a cough		
	kashyel'	кашель
cramps		
	spazmi	спазмы
diabetes		
	diabyet	диабет
diarrhoea		
	panos	понос

an earache	
balit ukha	болит ухо
epilepsy	
epilyepsiya	эпилепсия
a fever	
tyempyeratura	температура
food poisoning	
atravlyeniye	отравление
frost bite	
atmarazheniye	отморожение
glandular fever	
zhelyezistaya	железистая
likharatka	лихорадка
a headache	
balit galava	болит голова
hepatitis	
gyepatit	гепатит
high blood pressure	
gipyertaniya	гипертония
indigestion	
nyesvaryeniye	несварение
zhelutka	желудка
an infection	
infyektsiya	инфекция
influenza	
grip	грипп
insomnia	
byesonitsa	бессонница
an itch	
zut	зуд

lice
fshi
вши

low blood pressure
panizhenaye
davlyeniye
пониженное
давление

a pain here
balit tut
болит тут

a rash
sip'
сыпь

a sore throat
balit gorla
болит горло

a sprain
rastyazheniye
растяжение

a stomachache
balit zheludak
болит желудок

a temperature
tyempyeratura
температура

toothache
balit zup
болит зуб

venereal disease
vyenyerichyeskaya
balyezn'
венерическая
болезнь

worms
glista
глиста

I feel nauseous.
  myenya tashnit
                     Меня тошнит.
I keep vomiting.
  myenya rvyot
                     Меня рвёт.
I feel dizzy.
  u myenya kruzhitsa
  galava
                     У меня кружится
                     голова.

It started when I ...
  nachalos', kagda ya ...
                     Началось, когда ...
    ate (fish)
      syela (f)/*syel* (m)
      (ribu)
                 съела (f)/съел (m)
                 (рыбу).
    drank (water)
      vipila (f)/*vipil* (m)
      (vodu)
                 выпила (f)/
                 выпил (m) (воду).

I'm allergic to ...
  u myenya alyergiya k ...
                     У меня аллергия к ...
    antibiotics
      antibiotikam
                 антибиотикам
    penicilin
      pyenitsilinu
                 пенициллину

I have been vaccinated.
  mnye zdyelali privifku
                     Мне сделали
                     прививку.
I have my own needle.
  u myenya svoy
  sopstveniy shprits
                     У меня свой
                     собственный шприц.

What is the matter?
  shto samnoy?   Что со мной?
Is it serious?
  eta syer'yozna?   Это серьёзно?

Parts of the Body

arm
  ruka   рука
back
  spina   спина
blood
  krof'   кровь
breast
  grud'   грудь
chest
  grud'   грудь
ear(s)
  ukha (ushi)   ухо (уши)
eye
  glas (glaza)   глаз (глаза)
finger
  palyets   палец
foot
  naga   нога
hand
  ruka   рука
head
  galava   голова
heart
  syertse   сердце

knee
  kalyena   колено
kidney(s)
  pochka (pochki)   почка (почки)
leg
  naga   нога
liver
  pyechyen'   печень
mouth
  rot   рот
nose
  nos   нос
shoulder
  plyecho   плечо
teeth
  zup   зуб
throat
  gorla   горло
tongue
  yazik   язык

Pharmaceuticals

Do you have ...?
u vas yest' ...?   У вас есть ...?

aspirin
  aspirin   аспирин

baby powder
  pudra dlya ryebyonka   пудра для ребёнка

Band-aids
  plastir'   пластырь

a bandage
  bint   бинт

something for a cold
  shtonibud'   что-нибудь от
  atnasmarka   насморка

comb
  gryebyonka   гребёнка

condoms
  kandomi   кондомы

contraceptives
  prativazachatachniye противозачаточ-
  sryetstva   ные средства

cough mixture
  mikstura atkashlya   микстура
                     от кашля

deodorant
  sryetstva at pota   средство от пота

disinfectant
  dyezinfitsiruyushyeye дезинфицирую-
  sryetstva   щее средство

hairbrush
  shyotka dlya volas   щётка для волос

insect repellent
sryetstva at nasyekomikh
средство от насекомых

something for a headache
shto-nibut' ad galovnay boli
что-нибудь от головной боли

lozenges
tablyetki dlya gorla
таблетки для горла

moisturising cream
kryem dlya litsa
крем для лица

nail clippers
kusachki
кусачки

nappies
pyelyonki
пелёнки

needle
igolku
иголку

razor (disposable razors)
britvu (britvi dlya adnavo raza)
бритву (бритвы для одного раза)

razor-blades
lyezviya
лезвия

sanitary napkins
gigiyenichyeskiye salfyetki
гигиенические салфетки

shampoo
shampun'
шампунь

shaving cream
kryem dlya brit'ya
крем для бритья

soap
mila
мыло

talcum powder
tal'k   тальк
tampons
tamponi   тампоны
tissues
bumazhniye platki   бумажные платки
toilet paper
tualyetnuyu bumagu   туалетную бумагу
toothbrush
zubnuyu shyotku   зубную щётку
toothpaste
zubnuyu pastu   зубную пасту

Can you fix these glasses?
vi mozhetye pachinit'   Вы можете починить
mai achki?   мои очки?
When will they be ready?
kagda ani budut   Когда они будут
gatovi?   готовы?

Please make up this
prescription.
prigatof'tye, pazhalsta,   Приготовьте,
etat ryetsept   пожалуйста, этот
                                           рецепт.

When will it be ready?
kagda lyekarstva   Когда лекарство
budyet gatova?   будет готово?
How many times a day?
skol'ka raz v dyen'?   Сколько раз в день?

Some Useful Words

accident
  nyeshasniy sluchay несчастный случай
addiction
  narkamaniya наркомания
AIDS
  spit СПИД
antibiotics
  antibiotiki антибиотики
antiseptic
  antisyeptik антисептик
bite
  ukus укус
bleeding
  kravatyechyeniye кровотечение
blood pressure
  davlyeniye давление
blood test
  analis krovi анализ крови
injection
  inyektsiya инъекция
medication
  lyekarstva лекарство
menstruation
  myenstruatsiya менструация
(disposable) needle
  shprits (dlya adnavo шприц (для одного
  raza) раза)
ointment
  mas' мазь

pregnant
byeryemyenaya   беременная
prescription
ryetsept   рецепт
pills
pilyuli   пилюли
vitamins
vitamini   витамины
wound
ranyeniye   ранение

Times & Dates

Remember the all-purpose expression with times, dates and numbers:

Can you please write that
down?
   zapishitye eta,   Запишите это,
   pazhalsta   пожалуйста.

Telling the Time

Except for telling the time 'on the hour' (one o'clock, two o'clock, etc), the easiest and most precise way to tell the time in Russian is to say the hour, and then the minutes, as in English; eg 'eight forty-two'. You will also notice when reading timetables that Russians often use the twenty-four hour clock; therefore 'fourteen twenty' means 'twenty past two in the afternoon'.

What time is it?
   katoriy chas?   Который час?

Could you please show me
your watch?

pakazhitye, pazhalsta,
vashi chasi

Покажите, пожалуйста,
ваши часы.

1 o'clock
chas

Час

2 o'clock
dva chasa

Два часа

3 o'clock
tri chasa

Три часа

4 o'clock
chyetiri chasa

Четыре часа

5 o'clock
pyat' chasov

Пять часов

6 o'clock
shest' chasov

Шесть часов

7 o'clock
syem' chasov

Семь часов

8 o'clock
vosyem' chasov

Восемь часов

9 o'clock
dyevyat' chasov

Девять часов

10 o'clock
dyesyat' chasov

Десять часов

11 o'clock
adinatsat' chasov

Одиннадцать часов

12 o'clock
dvyenatsat' chasov.

Двенадцать часов

am
  utra   утра
pm
  dnya (in the afternoon)   дня
  vyechyera (in the evening)   вечера

You don't need to put in any word for 'it is' (a certain time):

It's 2.10 pm. (literally 'Fourteen ten')
  chyetirnatsat'   Четырнадцать
  dyesyat'   десять.

Note that if the minutes are under ten you need to insert the word
for 'zero', *nol'*, НОЛЬ:

It's 2.08 pm (literally
'fourteen zero eight')
  chyetirnatsat'   Четырнадцать
  nol' vosyem   ноль восемь.

in the ...
  morning
    utram   утром
  afternoon
    poslye abyeda   после обеда
  evening
    vyechyeram   вечером
  night
    noch'yu   ночью

at
  v   в

When ...?
  kagda...?   Когда ...?
    does it open
      atkrivayetsa   открывается
    does it shut
      zakrivayetsa   закрывается
    does it start
      nachinayetsa   начинается
    does it finish
      kanchayetsa   кончается

Days

On what day?
  f kakoy dyen'?   В какой день?
On what days (is the bank
shut)?
  f kakiye dni   В какие дни (банк
  (bank zakrit)?   закрыт)?

On ...
  v ...   В ...
    Monday
      panyedyel'nik   понедельник
    Tuesday
      ftornik   вторник
    Wednesday
      sryedu   среду

Thursday
  chyetvyerk   четверг
Friday
  pyatnitsu   пятницу
Saturday
  subotu   субботу
Sunday
  vaskryesyen'e   воскресенье

Months

January
  yanvar'   январь
February
  fyevral'   февраль
March
  mart   март
April
  apryel'   апрель
May
  may   май
June
  iyun'   июнь
July
  iyul'   июль
August
  avgust   август

September
  syentyabr'   сентябрь
October
  aktyabr'   октябрь
November
  nayabr'   ноябрь
December
  dyekabr'   декабрь

What is the date today?
  kakoye syevodnya   Какое сегодня
  chislo?   число?
On what date (are you
leaving)?
  kakova chisla   Какого числа (вы
  (vi uyezhayetye)?   уезжаете)?

When writing the date, Russians tend to put the month in Roman
numerals: 17 April 1994 will be 17/IV/94.

Present
today
  syevodnya   сегодня
this ...
    year
      vetam gadu   в этом году
    month
      vetam myesyatsye в этом месяце
    week
      na etoy nyedyelye на этой неделе

Past

yesterday
fchyera   вчера

the day before yesterday
pazafchyera   позавчера

last ...
- year
  f proshlam gadu   в прошлом году
- month
  f proshlam   в прошлом
  myesyatsye   месяце
- week
  na proshloy   на прошлой
  nyedyelye   неделе

Future

tomorrow
zaftra   завтра

the day after tomorrow
paslyezaftra   послезавтра

next ...
- year
  v budushyem gadu   в будущем году
- month
  v budushyem   в будущем
  myesyatsye   месяце
- week
  na budushyey   на будущей
  nyedyelye   неделе

Some Useful Words

(a year) ago
   (god) tamu nazat   (год) тому назад

always
   fsyegda   всегда

at the moment
   tyepyer'   теперь

century
   vyek   век

during
   vavryemya   во время

early
   rana   рано

every day
   kazhdiy dyen'   каждый день

for (time you intend being
somewhere)
   na   на

for the time being
   paka   пока

forever
   nafsyegda   навсегда

just then
(ie only minutes ago)
   tol'ka shto   только что

late
   pozna   поздно

later on
   patom   потом

never
   nikagda   никогда

not any more
   bol'she nyet   больше нет

not yet
   yeshyo nyet   ещё нет

now
   syeychas   сейчас

since
   s   с

sometimes
   inagda   иногда

sundown
   zakat   закат

sunrise
   rasvyet   рассвет

soon
   skora   скоро

still
   fsyo yeshyo   всё ещё

straight away
   syeychas   сейчас

used to
   ran'she   раньше

National Holidays

A handy expression for any special occasion:

Happy holiday!
   sprazbnikam!   С праздником!

At the moment there are days off for the following occasions:

New Year's Day (1 January) People have elaborate parties on
  New Year's Eve, and at midnight everyone toasts champagne
  and wishes 'Happy New Year!', *'snovim godam!'*, С НОВЫМ
  ГОДОМ! Greetings telegrams are more popular than cards.
  Children look forward to presents from Grandfather Frost, who
  is similar to Santa Claus.
International Women's Day (8 March) Russians also call this
  'Mothers' Day'. On this day men give flowers to women, and
  may cook dinner, to make up for the fact that life is generally
  miserable for Russian women. Most of the terrible frustrations
  we hear about, like queues and lack of facilities, are borne by
  women.

International Workers' Solidarity Day (1 May; 2 May is also a holiday) This is a day of official parades. Christians sometimes use this time to celebrate Easter.

Victory Day (9 May) This day commemorates the victory over the Nazis. Twenty million people in the USSR were killed during the war, and it is still an important memory. Even if you are cynical about the Government's motives in reminding people, it could be very offensive to say so.

Constitution Day (7 October)

Anniversary of the Great October Socialist Revolution (7 November; 8 November is also a holiday) This takes place in November, for before the Revolution, Russia used a different (Julian) calendar. The Tsar was actually overthrown earlier in 1917, and the Bolsheviks then seized power from the provisional government.

Numbers & Amounts

Numbers

How many?
 skol'ka? Сколько?

1	*adin*	один
2	*dva*	два
3	*tri*	три
4	*chyetiri*	четыре
5	*pyat'*	пять
6	*shest'*	шесть
7	*syem'*	семь
8	*vosyem'*	восемь
9	*dyevyat'*	девять
10	*dyesyat'*	десять
11	*adinatsat'*	одиннадцать
12	*dvyenatsat'*	двенадцать
13	*trinatsat'*	тринадцать
14	*chyetirnatsat'*	четырнадцать
15	*pyatnatsat'*	пятнадцать
16	*shesnatsat'*	шестнадцать
17	*syemnatsat'*	семнадцать
18	*vasyemnatsat'*	восемнадцать
19	*dyevyatnatsat'*	девятнадцать
20	*dvatsat'*	двадцать
21	*dvatsat' adin*	двадцать один
30	*tritsat'*	тридцать

40	*sorak*	сорок
50	*pidyesyat'*	пятьдесят
60	*shest'dyesyat'*	шестьдесят
70	*syem'dyesyat'*	семьдесят
80	*vosyem'dyesyat'*	восемьдесят
90	*dyevyanosta*	девяносто
100	*sto*	сто
134	*sto tritsat' pyat'*	тридцать сто пять
200	*dvyesti*	двести
300	*trista*	триста
400	*chetiryesta*	четыреста
500	*pyat'sot*	пятьсот
600	*shest'sot*	шестьсот
700	*syem'sot*	семьсот
800	*vasyem'sot*	восемьсот
900	*dyevyat'sot*	девятьсот
1000	*tisyacha*	тысяча

one million
  milion   миллион
two million
  dva miliona   два миллиона
zero
  nol'   ноль

If you're asking for a specific amount in a shop – such as 'ten, please' – Russians put a word that means something like 'items' after the numeral – 'ten items, please'. The word is *shtuki*, ШТУКИ, after 2 (in this context *dvye*, ДВЕ), 3 and 4; and *shtuk*, ШТУК, after 5 and above.

Three, please.
*tri **shtuki**, pazhalsta* Три штуки,
 пожалуйста.

Eight, please.
vosyem' shtuk, Восемь штук,
pazhalsta пожалуйста.

Fractions

$1/4$	*chyetvyert'*	четверть
$1/3$	*tryet'*	треть
$1/2$	*palavina*	половина
$3/4$	*tri chyetvyerti*	три четверти
$2/3$	*dvye **tryeti***	две трети

Ordinal Numbers

1st	*pyerviy*	первый
2nd	*ftaroy*	второй
3rd	*tryetiy*	третий
4th	*chyetvyortiy*	четвёртый
5th	*pyatiy*	пятый
6th	*shestoy*	шестой
7th	*syed'moy*	седьмой
8th	*vas'moy*	восьмой
9th	*dyevyatiy*	девятый
10th	*dyesyatiy*	десятый
20th	*dvatsatiy*	двадцатый
21st	*dvatsat' pyerviy*	двадцать первый

Amounts

How much?/ How many?
   skol'ka?   Сколько?

Could you please give me ...
   daytye, pazhalsta, ...   Дайте, пожалуйста, ...

I need ...
   *mnye **nada** ...*   Мне надо ...

   a bottle
      butilku   бутылку

   half a kg
      polkilo   полкило

   100 grams
      sto gram   сто грамм

   a jar
      banku   банку

   a kg
      kilo   кило

   a packet
      pakyet   пакет

   a slice
      kusok   кусок

   a tin
      banku   банку

Some Useful Words

enough
  dastatachna — достаточно
less
  myenshe — меньше
(just) a little
  (tol'ka) nyemnoshka — (только) немножко
many, much, a lot
  mnoga — много
too many, too much
  slishkam mnoga — слишком много
more
  bol'she — больше
some
  nyemnoga — немного

Vocabulary

Essential words you will need are included within this book, in the specific chapters. Here are some extra words that you may find useful as you get to know the language and the people of the USSR.

A

acupuncture
  akupunktura   акупунктура
addict
  narkaman   наркоман
all
  fsye   все
all of us
  mi fsye   мы все
alternative
  al' tyernativa   альтернатива
amusement park
  atraktsioni   аттракционы
annoyance
  dasada   досада
armaments
  varuzheniye   вооружение
army
  armiya   армия
art
  iskustva   искусство

atheist
  atyeist   атеист
(It's) awful
  kashmar   кошмар

B

babysitter
  prikhadyashaya nyanya   приходящая няня
ballet
  balyet   балет
Baltic States (the)
  pribaltika   Прибалтика
believe (v)
  vyerit'   верить
believer
  vyeruyushaya (f)   верующая (f)
  vyeruyushiy (m)   верующий (m)
better
  luchshe   лучше
Bible
  bibliya   Библия
birthday
  dyen' razhdyeniya   день рождения
boring
  skuchniy   скучный
botanical garden
  batanichyeskiy sat   ботанический сад

C

calculator
mikrokal'kulyatar микрокалькулятор

careful
vnimatyel'niy внимательный

cassette
kasyeta кассета

central
tsentral'niy центральный

Central Asia
sryednyaya aziya Средняя Азия

Cheers!
za vashe zdarov'ye! За ваше здоровье!

chess
shakhmati шахматы

child (for a)
dlya ryebyonka для ребёнка

cigarette (Western style)
sigaryeta сигарета

cigarette (Russian style)
papirosa папироса

citizen
grazhdanka (f) гражданка (f)
grazhdanin (m) гражданин (m)

communist
kamunistka (f) коммунистка (f)
kamunist (m) коммунист (m)

compact disc
kompakt disk компакт-диск

computer
   kamp'yutyer   компьютер
concert
   kantsert   концерт
Congratulations!
   pazdravlyayu!   Поздравляю!
contact lens(es)
   kantaktnaya linza   контактная линза
   (kantaktniye linzi)   (контактные линзы)
contraceptives
   prativazachatachniye   противозачаточные
   sryedstva   средства
cooperative
   kaapyerativ   кооператив
country (nation)
   strana   страна
country (in the)
   zagaradam   за городом
coupon
   talon   талон
crazy
   sumashetshiy   сумасшедший
creche
   yasli   ясли
credit card
   kryeditnaya kartachka   кредитная карточка

D
democracy
   dyemakratiya   демократия

dictionary
   slavar' словарь
dictionary (English-Russian)
   angla-ruskiy slavar' англо-русский словарь
dictionary (Russian-English)
   ruska-angliyskiy русско-английский
   slavar' словарь
disco
   diskatyeka дискотека
discrimination
   diskriminatsiya дискриминация
dream (n)
   son сон
drugs (illegal)
   narkotiki наркотики
drunk
   p'yaniy пьяный

E

economy
   khazyaystva хозяйство
emigrate (v)
   emigriravat' эмигрировать
the environment
   akruzhayushaya sryeda окружающая среда
exchange rate
   valyutniy kurs валютный курс
exhibition
   vistafka выставка

F

factory
  fabrika   фабрика
fault (It's not my)
  ya nye vinavata (f)   Я не виновата. (f)
  ya nye vinavat (m)   Я не виноват. (m)
film
  fil'm   фильм
fragile
  khrupkiy   хрупкий
funny
  smyeshnoy   смешной

G

garden
  sat   сад
glass of water
  stakan vadi   стакан воды
glass of wine
  ryumka vina   рюмка вина
glasses
  achki   очки
government
  pravityel'stva   правительство
guidebook
  putyevadityel'   путеводитель
guided tour
  ekskursiya   экскурсия
gynaecologist
  ginyekolag   гинеколог

H

hitchhike
yekhat' aftastopam ехать автостопом
home (at)
doma дома
hypnotism
gipnatizm гипнотизм

I

identification
dakumyenti документы
if
yesli если
inflation
inflyatsiya инфляция
(It's) impossible
nyevazmozhna Невозможно
interesting
intyeryesniy интересный
interpreter
pyeryevotchik переводчик
invitation
priglasheniye приглашение

K

king
karol' король
Koran
karan Коран

L

lens
abyektif — объектив
lost-property office
byuro nakhodak — бюро находок
love (to be in)
lyubit' — любить

M

make-up
kasmyetika — косметика
manager
administratar — администратор
modern
savryemyeniy — современный
music
muzika — музыка
music (classical)
klasichyeskaya muzika — классическая музыка
music (dance)
tantseval'naya muzika — танцевальная музыка
music (popular)
papulyarnaya muzika — популярная музыка
music (rock)
rokmuzika — рок-музыка

N

nothing
nichyevo — ничего

nuclear
  yadyerniy   ядерный
nuclear waste
  atkhodi atamnay   отходы атомной
  pramishlyenasti   промышленности

O

off (food)
  tukhliy   тухлый
offensive
  abidniy   обидный
Okay!
  kharasho!   Хорошо!
old-fashioned
  staramodniy   старомодный
opera
  opyera   опера
operation
  apyeratsiya   операция

P

party (get-together)
  vyechyerinka   вечеринка
Party (Communist)
  partiya   партия
  (kamunistichyeskaya)   (Коммунистическая)
peace
  mir   мир

pension (on a/the)
na pyensi   на пенсии
performer/celebrity
artistka (f)   артистка (f)
artist (m)   артист (m)
permission
razryesheniye   разрешение
personal
lichniy   личный
petrol
byenzin   бензин
petrol station
byenzakalonka   бензоколонка
play (performance)
p'yesa   пьеса
play (chess)
igrat' (f karti)   играть (в карты)
pollution
zagryaznyeniye   загрязнение
president
pryezidyent   президент
prime minister
pryem'yer-ministr   премьер-министр
private
chastniy   частный

Q
queen
karalyeva   королева

R

rationed
  patalonam   по талонам
revolution
  ryevalyutsiya   революция
rip-off
  abdiralafka   обдираловка
romantic
  ramantichyeskiy   романтический
rubbish
  musar   мусор

S

salary
  zarplata   зарплата
Siberia
  sibir'   Сибирь
skates
  kan'ki   коньки
skis
  lizhi   лыжи
state (belongs to government)
  gasudarstvyeniy   государственный
stereo system
  styeryeo-sistyema   стерео-система

T

tipsy
  pat khmyel'kom   под хмельком

Torah
   tora   Тора
trade union
   prafsayus   профсоюз

U

uncomfortable
   nyeudobniy   неудобный
unemployed
   byezrabotniy   безработный
unfair! (That's)
   eta nyespravyedliva!   Это несправедливо!
unfortunately
   k sazhalyeniyu   к сожалению
urgent
   srochniy   срочный

W

war
   vayna   война
war (civil)
   grazhdanskaya vayna   гражданская война
West (in the)
   na zapadye   на Западе
wonderful
   pryekrasniy   прекрасный

Z

zoo
   zaapark   зоопарк

Emergencies

Help!
na pomash!
На помощь!

Watch out!
astarozhna!
Осторожно!

Go away!
iditye atsyuda!
Идите отсюда!

Get lost!
pashol!
Пошёл!

Stop it (or I'll scream)!
*pyeryestan'
(a ta zakrichu)!*
Перестань (а то
закричу)!

Police!
militsiya!
Милиция!

Stop thief!
dyerzhitye vora!
Держите вора!

Call a doctor!
pazavitye vracha!
Позовите врача!

There's been an accident.
*praizashol nyeshasniy
sluchay*
Произошёл
несчастный случай.

Call an ambulance.
*vizavitye skoruyu
pomash'*
Вызовите скорую
помощь.

I am ill.
ya bal'na (f)/
ya bolyen (m)
Я больна (f)/
Я болен (m).

I am lost.
  ya patyeryalas' (f)/   Я потерялась (f)/
  ya patyeryalsa (m)   Я потерялся (m).

I've been raped.
  myenya iznasilavali   Меня износиловали.

I've been robbed.
  myenya agrabili   Меня ограбили.

I've lost my ...
  ya patyeryala (f)/   Я потеряла (f)/
  ya patyeryal (m)...   Я потерял (m)...
    bag
      sumku   сумку
    money
      dyen'gi   деньги
    travellers' cheques
      darozhniye chyeki   дорожные чеки
    passport
      paspart   паспорт

Could I use the telephone?
  mozhna   Можно
  vaspol'zavat'sa   воспользоваться
  vashim tyelyefonam?   вашим телефоном?

I have medical insurance.
  u myenya yest'   У меня есть
  myeditsinskaye   медицинское
  strakhavaniye   страхование.

USSR
a travel survival kit

Invaluable advice on getting around and beating red tape for individual and group travellers alike. This comprehensive guide includes an unsanitised historical background and complete information on arts and culture. It has over 130 reliable maps, and all place names are given in Cyrillic script.

Where Can You Find Out.........

HOW to get a Laotian visa in Bangkok?

WHERE to go birdwatching in PNG?

WHAT to expect from the police if you're robbed in Peru?

WHEN you can go to see cow races in Australia?

In the Lonely Planet Newsletter!

Every issue includes:

- *a letter from Lonely Planet founders Tony and Maureen Wheeler*
- *a letter from an author 'on the road'*
- *the most entertaining or informative reader's letter we've received*
- *the latest news on new and forthcoming releases from Lonely Planet*
- *and all the latest travel news from all over the world*

To receive the FREE quarterly Lonely Planet Newsletter, write to:
Lonely Planet Publications Pty Ltd (A.C.N. 005 607 983)
PO Box 617, Hawthorn, Vic 3122, Australia
Lonely Planet Publications, Inc
PO Box 2001A, Berkeley, CA 94702, USA